THE RISE OF T

It is more exciting tha...
thrilling to see a human...
ceremony, the chanting o...
of incense, the holiness of the proceedings has a comforting
effect. All has been sanctified by these things.

There would be a feeling too of exultation, and because it was
vaguely tinged with apprehension it would be the more exciting
for that. The Inquisitors were indefatigable ...

When would the next pall of smoke rise above the field which
had become the *quemadero*? When would they again have such
fun, throwing refuse at the prisoners and burning their beards?
When would they hear again those cries of anguish? And who
would be the next victims?

Also by Jean Plaidy in *Star*:

MARY QUEEN OF SCOTS: THE FAIR DEVIL OF SCOTLAND

To be published shortly:
THE GROWTH OF THE SPANISH INQUISITION
THE END OF THE SPANISH INQUISITION

THE RISE OF THE
SPANISH INQUISITION

Jean Plaidy

A STAR BOOK
published by
the Paperback Division of
W. H. ALLEN & Co. Ltd

A Star Book
Published in 1978
by the Paperback Division of
W. H. Allen & Co. Ltd
A Howard and Wyndham Company
44 Hill Street, London W1X 8LB

First published in Great Britain by
Robert Hale & Company, 1959

Copyright © Jean Plaidy 1959

Printed in Great Britain by
Cox & Wyman Ltd., London, Reading and Fakenham

ISBN 0 352 302119

NOTE

In order to avoid footnotes, sources and references are given
in the text.

My very special thanks are due to the librarians of Kensing-
ton Public Library who have worked so hard and patiently to
procure rare books for me, and thus have aided me considerably in my research.

CONTENTS

CHAPTER ONE

INTRODUCTION

It is sad and sobering to contemplate the torture which has been inflicted, the blood which has been shed in the name of Christ; and out of this contemplation arises an inevitable question: If the good and evil which have grown out of the Christian Religion could be weighed against one another, which would tip the scales?

It is important, I submit, to remember that Christianity and the Church do not always walk in step. In fact the simple doctrines, founded on the teachings of Jesus Christ, have too rarely been followed. They are too simple to appeal to men who love power and wealth – but mostly power – and how can men acquire power by following the doctrines of Christ? What temporal glory could they find in taking staff and scrip, divesting themselves of their worldly goods, and going forth to preach the simple doctrine: 'Love one another'?

Where in such a life were to be found the pomp and splendour, the ceremonial robes, the swaying censer, the fat incomes and the splendid palaces? Yet these were the signs of rank and importance necessary to induce that hypnotic state in which men might worship themselves whilst feigning to worship God.

Christ's doctrine was easy to teach, though by no means easy to carry out; and what was wanted by these seekers after power was a way of life difficult to teach and easy to live. Such a doctrine must therefore be attended by legends to make men's flesh creep; fear was necessary to a religion which was to bring power to its leaders, for fear is the complement of power. Men seek power to gain their objective and to overawe their fellows; and simplicity must be disguised by mysticism for the glorification of the high priests of power.

Thus, the simple doctrine was wrapped round and round

with dogma so involved that the seed which had been planted by Jesus Christ was hidden and forgotten; taking the place of the wandering teacher who had given up all his worldly goods to the poor and followed in his Master's footsteps, there were the powerful men of the Church.

But the men of the Church could not agree, and since the dogmas and doctrines were of greater importance to them than the words of Jesus Christ, they fought amongst themselves, seeking to enforce their rule upon each other. Yet they did not altogether forget their Master for constantly they invoked His Name. Thousands were submitted to the cruellest torture these men could devise; the flesh of their victims was torn with red hot pincers, and molten lead poured into the wounds; many suffered the agonies of the hoist and the water torture; some were racked to death; some were burned at the stake; every means of dealing pain and indignity to the human body was explored; and all this was done in the name of One who had commanded his followers to love one another.

There must have been many – Jews and Moslems – who fervently wished that Jesus Christ had never made His appearance on Earth, when contemplating all the misery which would have been spared them, their families and friends, but for this, to them, calamitious event. This will be considered a shocking statement – and indeed it is. But it is a true one and therein lies the horror of it.

The Inquisition was surely one of the most cruel institutions ever set up by man, and it is interesting to study it in relation to the history of that country which embraced it most fervently. It was an evil thing and from it grew evil. The comparative religious tolerance displayed by Spain's great rival – England – was in some measure the cause of that rival's success, to the detriment of Spain. The known world was too small to contain two mighty seafaring colonizers; and it was those whose main intention was to trade, who scored over those who went to extend the Catholic world with the help of instruments of torture.

No great Empire has yet achieved permanence, and we who are witnessing the dissolution of one of the greatest, are unable at this stage to understand exactly where it failed. History is like a picture that must be looked at from a distance; it is like a vast oil painting; and the brilliant figures, which seem to dominate it when we stand close to it, in the long view may appear to be of lesser importance.

It is nearly five hundred years since Isabella and Ferdinand brought the Inquisition into their territory; so that the picture on which we can look back is a clear one. We can see the conquistadors going forth with patriotic valour in their hearts and the rack and the bilboes in their ships; we can see the expulsion of the Jewish race from Spain; we can see the folly of trying to force an unwanted religion on natives who were less inclined to hate the explorer if he came to trade and not to destroy their gods; we can see the even greater folly of expelling those men who, throughout the ages, have made rich the countries they inhabit. Thus, the Inquisition abroad brought bloodshed and misery to thousands and sowed the seeds of hatred instead of love, while the Inquisition in Spain robbed the country of the men who made it rich. Persecution of the Jews has always been one of the most foolish policies any country can pursue. Not only is persecution an evil thing, but also a very stupid one.

It may be said that the greatest disaster Spain suffered was in the year 1588 off the coast of Britain; although it is fashionable now to state that it was not the genius of Drake, Effingham, and the English sailors, which defeated the 'Invincible Armada', but the inclemency of the English climate. Quite clearly it was the fine fighting spirit of the English sailors and the English people which defeated the Armada although the storms came after the battle and completed the victory. But the determination to hold off the invader was surely the fiercer because it was known throughout the land that with the fighting ships, came also the ships of the Inquisition, and that it was Philip's intention to set up the dreaded monster in our islands. Therefore, this major defeat of a country, which was until that time the mightiest in the world, was in some measure due to the Inquisition.

My plan is to study this hideous monster, to expose it in all its horror, to try to understand the motives of those who installed it and those who fought against it. For this purpose I want to look at the country which embraced it so whole-

9

heartedly, at the origins, the ignoble existence and the end of this institution which called itself the 'Holy Office' and operated in the name of Jesus Christ who had commanded His followers to love one another.

CHAPTER TWO

BEGINNINGS

When in the twelfth century Pope Innocent III commanded members of the Church to persecute suspected heretics, he heralded the birth of the Inquisition, although this was not firmly established as such until the reign of Pope Gregory IX. The term *inquisitio* was already known; but before the twelfth century heretics were rarely burned to death for refusing to adopt the doctrines of the Catholic Church, and were usually punished by confiscation of their property.

Deanesly, in his *A History of the Medieval Church 590–1500* recalls one instance in 1075 of a Catharist's being put into a shed which was set on fire; and another which took place in 1114, when an enraged mob took heretics from a prison and burned them alive; but it was only when the Catholic Church began to see danger in allowing men to live who supported a doctrine different from their own, that the great Inquisition was founded.

It has been said that the zealots of the Inquisition, even in their acts of greatest cruelty, believed themselves to be justified in what they did. We are asked to accept as a fact that they were deeply religious men who honestly and sincerely believed that they were serving God in what they did. We are told that they believed heretics were destined for eternal damnation, and that it was their duty to save them from that, no matter what pain they inflicted on the bodies of these heretics here on Earth. Those who would have us believe that the Inquisition was in itself evil, but kept the Catholic Church in existence despite those who sought to destroy it, tell us that the Inquisitors believed that while the bodies of unrepentant heretics were being consumed by the flames, they would be given – as nothing else could give them – a taste of what perpetual hellfire would be like. Thus, declared the supporters of the Inquisition, in their last moments of life on Earth, might these lost men and women save their souls for God – saved 'yet as by fire'.

It is a plausible excuse; but we must remember that it was fear of the heretic which inspired the foundation of the Inquisition; and that its victims were more likely to be rich men, whose goods were worthy of confiscation, than men whose worldly goods were few.

There may have been some who believed that they were obeying the Divine Will by spreading fear throughout the land and torturing their fellow men; but if we excuse these men their simple-mindedness, we must condemn their stupid arrogance, for it is surely the height of stupidity to persecute those who do not think as ourselves; and when this is a matter of 'Faith', surely the condemnation is doubly arrogant.

The very word heresy, derived as it is from the Greek *Hairesis*, 'choice', might – had these persecutors been possessed of one little streak of that humility, without which real wisdom cannot be acquired – have made them pause to ask themselves how they dared interfere in such a brutal way with the considered conclusions to which other men had come. But these persecutors had placed themselves outside the world of logic, as all who possess blind faith, and believe there is virtue in possessing this, must be; they were not even prepared to pity those who lacked it; they were going to castigate them; they submitted them to the most acute mental and physical torture they could contrive; and all because they did not accept the dogma which they in their blind faith accepted.

Persecution there has always been but, in the early history of religion when men might be expected to be less civilized, there was never any persecution to compare with the horrors of the Inquisition. A great deal has been written about Roman persecution of the Christian martyrs, but it is said that the number of victims sacrificed to the Inquisition in the reign of Philip II of Spain exceeded by many thousands those who died at the order of the Emperors of Rome. Moreover, the Roman Emperors worshipped Pagan gods; they had not been commanded to love one another.

It has often been stated that the early Christians might have lived in peace, pursuing their own religious beliefs, had they been inclined to do so; yet it seems that these men and women were so zealous, so determined to convert all those with whom they came into contact, or denounce them as heathen, that they brought upon themselves the ire of the Roman community; they refused to serve in the armies, declaring that it was forbidden for a Christian to kill his fellow men. (What a pity Christians did not remember this in the centuries to come!) Such conduct was certain to bring trouble upon them and may have been one of the reasons why they were thrown to the lions for the entertainment of the Romans.

Claudius expelled them as undesirables; Nero and Domitian were less lenient but, when the wife of the latter arranged for his removal in the year 96 and the just Nerva was elected by the Senate, a new age of tolerance began, and this wise Emperor made Christians welcome in Rome and forbade persecution on the ground of religion. Marcus Ulpius Trajan, who became Nerva's successor was, perhaps, less tolerant; he declared the Christians to be a political danger, yet he did not allow them to be persecuted on account of their beliefs, but with the coming of Marcus Aurelius Antoninus, the Stoic and philosopher, came a new era of persecution for the Christians which was in its turn to be replaced by a more tolerant one.

It seems possible that, had the early Christians been content to obey the Master's simple instructions, they would not have suffered so intensely as martyrs. Had they been content to love each other, would they have been prevented from doing so? Perhaps, had they carried out the simple instructions, those about them would have noticed the admirable example they set, and have wished to emulate them. This might have resulted in a spreading of real Christianity, as no amount of preaching or martyrdom could do. But the creed was too simply stated, too difficult to follow. They must have their meetings, their little pomps, their rites; and since they would, during the years of persecution, have been forced to meet in secret, they were naturally suspected and marked as dangerous political enemies of Romans. They were brave men and women; but perhaps it was less difficult to live as they did – dangerously, excitingly – than to live the life of self-denial, loving their neighbours as they loved themselves.

Did these beginnings give them a contempt for life in general? If they risked their own they would surely be more ready to jeopardize the lives of others. The Christian Faith had been spread by many who had died the martyr's death. Was that why the Christian Faith imposed the martyr's death on others?

Intolerance appeared to be embodied in the Faith. Indeed, all those who sought to mould it and direct it were determined to cultivate and preserve intolerance. St Augustine who, I suppose more than any other man of the Church, directed it in the way it was to go, set the pattern for the future when he demanded: *Quid est enim pejor, mors animae quam libertas erroris*? He firmly believed that heretics should die, as their presence among the believers was a danger. It is a pity that this Bishop of Hippo, the most important of all the Fathers of the Church, should have taken as his mentor – as so many others did – St Paul rather than Jesus.

His predilection for the apostle rather than the Master was probably due to the fact that in his youth he had led a dissolute life. He was converted to the faith of his mother (St Monica) on reading in the Epistle of Paul the Apostle to the Romans:

'Let us walk honestly, as in the day; not in rioting and drunkenness, not in chambering and wantonness, not in strife and envying.
But put ye on the Lord Jesus Christ, and make not provision for the flesh, to fulfil the lusts thereof.'

Do those who have to subdue the lusts of the flesh, as did St Augustine and St Paul, in doing so suppress their finer feelings, their sensitivity? Are they conscious of a burning resentment against that which makes its demands on them, and while they are determined not to fall into temptation – and indeed succeed with a resolution which is admirable – do they feel a great desire to see others share their suffering, their frustration and their triumphs? These are the hard men; the men who build with determination, with fire, with zeal, but with bitterness, with stoical determination which leads them to say: 'I have suffered; so shall others suffer.'

Perhaps there would have been fewer blots on the Christian story if it had continued in the style of the Master instead of in the bitter pioneering of one of the Master's brave, religious but human followers.

From the fifth century – when the barbarian hordes put an end to the great Roman Empire – to the twelfth, while there had been few religious persecutions there had been men to question certain tenets of the Church, putting forward their own ideas and – as they considered – improvements. Among these were the Arians, the Catharists, the Gnostics, the Manichaeans, and the Waldenses.

Arius, who founded Arianism, was a priest of Alexandria who lived in the fourth century. The main tenet of Arianism was the denial of the consubstantiality of the Son with the Father in the Trinity. His theories were condemned in 325 and he was banished to Illyricum; his writings were destroyed and it was forbidden for any to possess them. However, the Emperor Constantine, who was later baptized as a Christian, relented and recalled Arius, who would have been taken back into the Church had he not died before this could be done. But his theories did not die with him, and a sect grew up which called itself Arian.

The Catharists or Cathari were puritanical in outlook; they were confirmed in the belief that all fleshly desire was sinful and sought to suppress these desires and mortify the flesh in order to cultivate purity.

The Gnostics believed that knowledge was more important than blind faith; and thus they began to question Christianity itself, expressing doubts as to whether Christ was God manifest in the flesh.

The Manichaeans believed that the world had been created not by God alone, but by two opposing influences: God which is spirit, and the Devil which is evil and matter. This idea was put forth by Manes who was a Persian and who died in the year A.D. 274; but it seems that it was not original since it was obviously borrowed from the theories set out by Zoroaster who founded the Parsee religion about 800 B.C.

The Waldenses were of much later origin, being founded in 1170 by Peter Waldo (or Pierre de Vaux) whose idea was to purge the Church of much which had been added during the past centuries and return to the original primitive doctrines. This sect was also known as the Vaudois; and naturally suffered great persecution.

It was the activities of these various sects in France which attracted the attention of Rome in the twelfth century.

France, habitually leading the world in intellectual matters, had for some years been casting about for ways to reform the Church. The North and the South were as different as if they had been two separate countries. North of the Loire, and the Rhone, the people were faithful to the orthodox Church, however much they craved for reform.

Peter Abélard was thundering forth from the Mount St Geneviéve and at the Paraclete, posing his scientific-religious questions for the Church to answer. These questions produced a certain amount of trepidation, for they threatened the simple faith which so far had been followed.

But there was that pillar of the Church, the Abbot of Clairvaux, St Bernard himself, to pit his wits against those of the fiery philosopher and to remind the people of this man's scandalous passion for Hélöise, the prioress of Argenteuil and Abbess of the Paraclete. St Bernard was the victor in this verbal duel and the teachings of Abélard were condemned at the Councils of Soissons and Sens, as a result of which Abélard was forbidden to lecture and forced to retire to the Abbey of St Marcellus, not far from Châlon-sur-Saône, that he might cause no more disturbance. The Holy Office had not yet been set up and there was no question of Abélard's burning at the stake because his opinions diverged from those of the Church. He was, on the contrary, received with great kindness by Peter the Venerable, Abbot of Cluni, and there he stayed until his death in 1142.

In the north of France the battle between Abélard and the

Church had been won by the Church. It was a different matter in the south.

The people of the south were of very mixed blood. There had been constant invasions over the centuries and mingling with the blood of Gaul was that of Rome; and there had been Arab, Visigothic and Asiatic infiltration. These people then had been made aware of many faiths; they were a highly civilized people accustomed to thinking for themselves; and it was in the south of France that the various sects were more numerous than in any other part of Europe.

These people were pleasure-loving and cultured. From such districts as Provence and Aquitaine came the troubadours and the poets. These were bold men and not of a temper to accept any faith blindly. Their rulers, lords of a district, such as the Count of Toulouse, were well satisfied with their way of life and made no attempt to interfere with the manner in which their subjects worshipped God. Indeed, they were accused of listening to those who sought to spread their different sects; and so interesting were these, and such favour did they find with so many people, that it came to the ears of the Pope Eugenius III that heresy was growing in the south of France and spreading beyond its borders.

St Bernard, fresh from his triumphs over Peter Abélard, decided to go to the south of France in order to turn the heretics from their evil ways; and taking with him Cardinal Albéric, the Papal legate, he set out. He was appalled by what he found. 'Churches without flocks, flocks without priests,' as he wrote; and he sought to harangue these pleasure-loving people of the south to achieve greater piety. He found them indifferent and when he preached in the church at Vertfeuil, many of the most important people of the district walked out; moreover when the more humble saw what their lords were doing, they did the same. St Bernard followed them into the streets, continuing with his sermon; but the people had determined not to be preached to; those who could disappear, did so; others knocked on the doors of the houses in unison, and there was such a clamour that St Bernard could not hear his own voice.

The incensed saint cursed the place, shouting in a far from saintly manner: 'Vertfeuil, God wither thee!'

Then he departed; but that was not the end of the campaign against the bold men of the south.

In the year 1165 the Council of Lombers was called together in the diocese of Albi, and the heretics of the south of France were publicly condemned; and from that time they were all known – whether they were Arians or Gnostics, Manichaeans or Catharists – as Albigenses, after the town of Albi in which the Council had met.

Persecutions were carried out but feebly during the next thirty years; the old Count of Toulouse, Raymond V, had died and his son, Raymond VI, was said to be even more lenient than his father had been. News of what was happening in the south of France filtered through to Rome, but nothing was done; and the Albigenses continued to live their pleasant lives, assembling to discuss religion, putting forward their newest theories, all under the benign protection of Raymond who was, according to Rome, infected with the new ideas.

In the year 1198 a new Pope was elected. This was Lotario de' Conti, who became Innocent III. Innocent was determined to stamp out heresy and spread the Holy Catholic Faith throughout the world. He had long been aware of how matters stood south of the Loire and he was determined to put an end to the *laissez-aller* policy of the last thirty years. He began by despatching missionaries to France. Before persecuting, he meant to persuade.

This, as in the case of St Bernard, met with little success. The rulers of the various districts, when asked why they allowed heretics to remain in their terrain, replied that these people whom the Pope's missionaries called heretics were those for whom they had great affection; they had been brought up with them; they had married into their families and they had discovered that their divergence from orthodox Christianity had in no way impaired their honesty. It was impossible to turn them out.

Meeting with what seemed to be indestructible opposition, the missionaries lost heart and asked to be allowed to give up the work. Among these was Peter de Castelnau, a man who had worked with great enthusiasm in an endeavour to drive heresy from the south of France.

Two Spanish priests who were travelling in France met the Papal missionaries in Montpellier, and they discussed at great length the difficulty of bringing about reform among the heretics; and the Spanish priests were appalled by the despondency of the missionaries.

One of these Spaniards was the Bishop of Osma, Diego d'Azevedo, and the other his sub-prior, a nobleman of Spain named Domingo de Guzman, who was afterwards to achieve great fame as St Dominic, the founder of the Dominicans who were to control the Inquisition.

During the discussions the Spaniards suggested that if the missionaries went among the heretics simply clad and on foot, as their Master had, they might make more impression on these people than by travelling, as they did at present, with all the pomp and splendour of Papal emissaries.

The weary missionaries were so discouraged by failure, that they were ready to try anything which might bring them success; but they insisted that they could not diverge so extraordinarily from custom unless they had the authority of a person of importance.

The Bishop of Osma remained in France with his sub-prior, de Guzman, sending his retinue back to Spain; and this matter of founding a mendicant order was discussed among priests and Papal missionaries until it so fired the young Domingo de Guzman that he determined to make the founding of such an order his life's work.

Dominic and Diego d'Azevedo worked among the Albigenses with great fervour, casting aside all splendour and going among them simply clad; but the Albigenses loved their troubadours and their poetry, their intellectual discussions, and they were no more impressed by the humble preachers than they had been by those who had come in splendour. All they desired was to be allowed to live in freedom, to give their minds full range. This was a state of affairs which had existed in the south of France for many years; they were determined that it should remain so.

Raymond VI was not a bold man; he was a lover of peace. He could not welcome the officials of the Church in his domain because he knew that they wished him to imprison and torture those who followed beliefs diverging from the Catholic Faith as set out by the Church. All Raymond asked was that life should go on pleasantly as it had in the last years.

When Peter de Castelnau found Raymond evasive, twisting words and arguments in such a manner that it became clear that he would not introduce stern measures against heretics in his domains, he was angry and demanded Raymond's excommunication. Innocent excommunicated Raymond and let him know that other dire penalties awaited him if he did not conform.

Raymond was now afraid; he prevaricated, sought for time; he made promises which he knew he would not keep, and indeed he did soon afterwards revoke them.

Castelnau, furious at this treatment, decided to return to Rome to assure the Pope that the only way in which Raymond could be dealt with was by fire and sword.

In January of the year 1208 the Legates, with Castelnau at their head, set out for Rome. They rested for a night at an inn on the banks of the Rhône and early next morning, as they were leaving, two men who had stayed the night at the same inn came towards them as though to speak in a friendly fashion; then one of them drew his sword and plunged it into the body of Peter de Castelnau.

Castelnau fell to the ground, crying out that he hoped God would forgive his murderer as he himself did. Then he died.

This was one of the greatest calamities which could have befallen the Albigenses and freedom of thought.

The Papal Legate had been murdered. This was a blow at the Pope, at the Church itself. It could not be ignored; and through it Innocent saw a way of rallying the whole Catholic world against the Albigenses of the south of France.

The man who was blamed for this outrage was Raymond VI of Toulouse, although he had not been present at the murder.

An event, which had taken place in England thirty years before in 1170, was recalled. Then the Archbishop of Canterbury, Thomas a'Becket, had fallen into a difference of opinion with his King, Henry II, because Becket was eager to preserve the independence of the Church. The King, it was believed, had been heard to murmur that he wished someone would rid him of this man; consequently the Archbishop had been murdered by four knights on the steps of the altar of Canterbury Cathedral. The point was that, although the King had not been present at the murder, it had been committed at his instigation; he realized his guilt and had done penance for the deed. As Henry II of England had been guilty of the murder of Thomas a'Becket, so was Raymond VI of Toulouse guilty of the murder of Peter de Castelnau.

This gave Innocent the excuse he needed. The Crusades, those holy wars under the banner of the Cross, the purpose of which was to recover the Holy Land from the Saracens, were still being carried on. In fact at this time the fourth Crusade (there were eight in all), which had been organized by Innocent himself, had just terminated. If, declared Innocent, good Christians made war on the Infidel in the Holy Land and received the blessing of God for so doing, how much more necessary was it to do God's work nearer home? These people in the south of France were even worse than the Infidel; for the Infidel was ignorant and had had no chance of coming to the true faith. It was therefore the duty of all lovers of the Church to act against them; and he commanded the King of France, Philip II (Philip-Augustus), with the nobles and clergy, to put on the cross and begin a crusade against the heretics of the South. Raymond of Toulouse was a greater scoundrel than Saladin, said Innocent, and the Albigenses more worthy of extermination than the Saracens.

Innocent was more than a religious fanatic; he was a good politician. While he called forth the wrath of Christianity against the Albigenses, he did not forget to offer their lands and other possessions to any who would conquer them. So he was sure of raising a large army.

Thus in the year 1208 began the war against the Albigenses which was to drag on for fifteen years and bring great misery to people who had asked for nothing but to be allowed to use their minds and state their opinions.

It was more than a wasteful, stupid war; for out of its misery and horror was born that monster: the Inquisition.

The man whose name is linked with that of Innocent III in

the war of the Church against the Albigenses is Simon, Count of Monfort-l'Amaury, the father of the famous Simon de Montfort who married the sister of Henry III of England and came into notorious conflict with that monarch. Simon the father was a French count, whose ancestor, the first Lord of Montfort, had possessed nothing but a little castle, situated between Paris and Chartres.

The family, however, prospered, and one of the lords of Montfort married the daughter of the Earl of Leicester, thus giving the family a stake in England. The fourth Earl of Leicester on his death left the Honour of Leicester to this daughter who had married the de Montfort and who was the mother of that Simon who distinguished himself in the war against the Albigenses. King John reluctantly recognized Simon as the Earl of Leicester, but later took an opportunity of seizing his estates; which were after a while restored but again confiscated.

It evidently became apparent to Simon that he would be wiser to throw in his lot with France than England, for this is what he did; and he took up residence among his Norman estates under Philip II of France (Philip-Augustus).

Simon took part in the Fourth Crusade against the Infidel and during this achieved great renown as a fine soldier and leader, a man entirely devoted to the establishing of the Catholic Faith among the Infidels.

With the death of Castelnau, Innocent, determined to carry war into the Albigenses' stronghold, saw in the return of Simon an opportunity too good to be missed; so he called upon the returning hero to take part in a new crusade, this time nearer home, in his own France against a people who, declared Innocent, needed the scourge even more than did the Infidels.

Thus in the year 1208 Simon de Montfort became Captain General of the army which waged war against the heretics.

His experience of battle, his fervour and his confidence that right was on his side, soon gained the victories he desired; and one by one the towns which the Albigenses defended fell into the hands of de Montfort.

In the battles against the Saracens the holy warriors had believed that no cruelty or indignity was too extreme to be indulged in; they were able to assure themselves that whatever they did was for the glory of God; and since they had made God in their own image, it was easy to imagine Him, sitting on His throne above, watching with approval their cruelty because it was all perpetrated in His honour. Simon was no exception, and in the towns of Carcassonne, Béziers, Toulouse and countless others, fanatical cruelty was carried out.

But the Albigenses were stubborn folk. Moreover there was more than freedom of thought to fight for; there was their property which the Pope had declared should be forfeited to the conquerors, and many of these towns which fell to the invading armies were won back and lost again; and so the war was to drag on, causing great misery to this beautiful country.

Simon, a true fanatic of his day, believed that the just punishment of heretics should be death by fire, and he did not fail to inflict this.

There is a story told of him that, after the battle of Castres, two heretics were brought forward for his judgement. One of these men, terrified at the prospect of the torture and terrible death which he knew waited those who fell into the hands of de Montfort, declared his willingness to be converted. The other, however, was a braver man and he definitely said that the tormentors could do what they would with his body; he would remain true to his beliefs.

De Montfort's reply was: 'Take them both to the stake and there let them suffer death by burning. If this man who declares his willingness to reform his ways speaks the truth, his fiery death will expiate the sin against God which he has committed by falling into heresy; and if he is lying, he will suffer the penalty for his deceit.'

No doubt he was busy, but one wonders how Catholic historians can write so fulsomely of a man who could lightly condemn, to one of the most horrible deaths conceived by man, a victim who expressed his willingness for conversion. The answer may be that, like so many such stories, this one is apocryphal. It may be so; but there is the terrible cruelty of the campaign against the Albigenses and the pillaging of that land of the Rhône, the Garonne and the Pyrenees with all the attendant horror and massacre, to bear witness to this bloody war which was carried on in the name of Holy Church.

When the Church's forces conquered the town of Béziers, Arnauld, Abbot of Cîteaux was so eager for the extirpation of the heretics that, on being told that many good Catholics resided in the city and asked how the soldiers should be able to differentiate between the faithful and traitors to the Church, he replied in his fanatical zeal: 'Slay all, for God will certainly know His own.'

So great was this man's desire to stamp out heresy that it seemed unimportant that a few of the faithful should be sacrificed in the attempt.

It is said that on that occasion twenty thousand men, women and children of the town of Béziers were killed.

Pierre de Vaulx-Cernay tells another story which throws a light on the manner in which the holy campaign was carried out, and this seems the place to relate it.

The seige of the Château de Lavaur had been broken in the year 1211, and the seigneur of the château was made a prisoner with about eighty of his followers and, probably because he was pressed for time, Simon de Montfort decided that they should be hanged on one gibbet. The seigneur was hanged, but the poles of the gallows, which had been erected in a hurry, broke; thereupon de Montfort, eager to go on to fresh conquests, ordered that the rest of the knights should be decapitated on the spot immediately. This was done. But the lady of the castle, who happened to be the sister of the seigneur, was noted for her heresy, and had committed the heinous crime, not only of practising it herself, but of spreading it; and it was decided that a very memorable example must be made of her. She was thrown into a well, and the holy men then showed their zeal for their faith by seeking as many large boulders as they could find and throwing them down the well after the lady.

The War of the Albigenses, in which the seeds of the Inquisition were first planted, soon ceased to be a war of religion; conquest under the cloak of religion was the aim of those who waged war in the name of the Church against the Albigenses.

How often in the history of the Inquisition were rich men seized because they were rich men rather than because they were heretics? Was the fury of the Holy Office directed against those Jews because they, having been forced to accept Christianity, were accused of reverting to their own faith, or because they were rich men whose goods could be confiscated by the Inquisition? There can be no clear-cut answer to this, for human motives were then, as always, mixed. But there can be no doubt that Simon de Montfort, while being a zealous follower of the faith, was also a very ambitious man. Even his apologists must admit that he lost few opportunities of enriching himself while he worked for the glory of the Church; and while he showed a great hatred of the heretic he could not hide an equally great love for their possessions.

It is interesting to remember that after the fall of Béziers and Carcassonne, when the land and treasure of Raymond Roger were to be shared among the conquerors, these were offered to the Duke of Burgundy, the Count of Nevers and the Count of St Paul. Now these Frenchmen must have felt some shame in robbing one of their own countrymen of his possessions, for they all declined the offer, declaring that they had lands enough of their own.

There was one, however, who did not share their delicate feelings. This was Simon de Montfort who lost no time in adding the title of Viscount of Béziers and Carcassonne to those he already possessed.

Raymond Roger was imprisoned in Carcassonne and three months later he was dead. It has been said that he was murdered, but it is by no means certain that this crime was committed by de Montfort.

The war against the Albigenses continued to drag on and it was still in progress in the summer of 1216 when Innocent died. Honorius III, his successor, lacked his reforming skill; much of the fire which had spurred on the crusaders in the beginning was lost, and the men of the south of France took fresh hope. It was then that the towns which they had lost fell into their hands once again; and two years after the death of Innocent, Simon de Montfort found himself outside the walls of Toulouse, making at attempt to recapture it. A shower of stones from the city's ramparts descended on him, unhorsing him and killing him.

So neither he nor Innocent saw the end of the war which they had begun. But when they had made war against the Albigenses, they had laid the foundations for the establishment of the Inquisition.

Innocent III has been called the greatest of the medieval Popes. He was thirty-seven at the time of his election, and we are told that he accepted the tiara with reluctance; though why this should have been so is hard to understand since he was clearly a very ambitious man and, as he had entered the Church, it seems unlikely that he would have been reluctant to achieve its highest office.

I think this reluctance, which is referred to again and again by Catholic writers (not only in the case of Innocent III, but in that of almost every Pope with the exception of those such as Alexander VI – Roderigo Borgia – whom it is impossible for the most determined recorder to whitewash) was a matter of lip service paid to the high office. Of course it may have been a point of etiquette to feign reluctance; but one is reminded of the case of Julius Caesar who was offered the crown three times, and who put it from him although he was 'very loth to lay his fingers off it.'

Innocent, then Lotario de' Conti, was the son of Count Trasimund of Segni; and Clement III was his uncle; so it may well have been that from childhood he was destined for high office in the Church. He prospered during the four brief reigns of Lucius III, Urban III, Gregory VIII and Clement III; but when Celestine III was elected to the Papal throne, it was necessary for Lotario to retire into obscurity, for Celestine was of the House of Orsini and the Orsinis were enemies of the Counts of Segni; so for seven years there was no hope of advancement for Lotario.

But on the death of Celestine he was elected Pope.

He was very young, and it is surprising that he should have been elected, for youth was certainly no asset in an election. There were many Cardinals who, although had the offer of the tiara been made to them would no doubt have shown the usual reluctance to take it, were very loth to lay their fingers off it. If these Cardinals failed to be elected it was always a matter of consolation to contemplate that before long there would be another Conclave and consequently another chance. That was why aged Popes were usually elected. The strength of Innocent's character must have been marked at this time, for it was a great achievement to be elected Pope at the age of thirty-seven. He died at 56, so he had a long session.

He was possessed of three great ambitions: to capture the Holy Land for Christendom, to make the Papacy supreme in Europe, and to wipe out heresy.

He could be said to have achieved some success in two of these desires. He very soon subdued the Italian peninsula which was at the time of his accession in the hands of German overlords; and before his death there were few countries in Europe which did not come under Papal influence. As for the last of his ambitions: on him falls the shame of having laid the foundation of the Inquisition. It was he who, during the first year of his reign, despatched the two Cistercian monks, Rainer and Guido into the south of France, there to hunt out heresy commanding all lords in the neighbourhood to give these 'inquisitors' all the help they should need. The failure of his emissaries was to result in the war against the Albigenses.

In 1209 he set up the Council of Avignon at which every bishop was ordered to gather together men of authority in his diocese and force them to swear that they would do all in their power to exterminate heretics.

Some five years later, in November of 1215, the Fourth Lateran Council took place. This is referred to by Michael Ott in his essay in the *Catholic Encyclopedia* as 'the culminating point in the glorious reign,' and 'the most important conference of the Middle Ages.' Its glory is doubtful; its importance is not disputed. At this gathering of Churchmen it was decided to launch a further Crusade to the Holy Land, and so further Innocent's great ambition to extirpate the Saracen and bring the Holy Land under Christian domination. This did not give the conference its significance in history; there had been other crusades. But during this meeting seventy decrees of a reformatory nature were issued. Among these was the creed *Firmiter*

26

Credimus, and all those in authority were commanded, if they would be considered faithful to the Church (and it was becoming more and more clear that it was dangerous for any man to be otherwise) to swear publicly that they would with all their might and with all their strength drive heresy from the face of the Earth.

This was not all; and here was that menace which was such an integral part of the Inquisition. A Bull was issued which informed the faithful that it was a crime *not* to extirpate heretics, and any discovered to be guilty of this crime would not only be excommunicated, but would himself be suspected of heresy.

Thus men were instructed to be not only faithful Catholics, not only haters of all those who held different views from their own; they must also become spies to carry tales of their neighbours, and perhaps – if there were nothing to report – to invent them; because a man who had nothing to tell might lay himself open to suspicion.

Thus the Lateran Council.

It is natural, looking back over the centuries, to view with repulsion any who would have had a hand in establishing the terrible Inquisition, but it would not be fair to dismiss Innocent as a cruel man because of the part he played in its establishment. Innocent is called, by Catholics who make light of the sufferings of heretics and often refer to the 'much maligned Inquisition', the greatest Pope of the Middle Ages; and from one point of view this was so.

Innocent was energetic; there is no doubt that he acted in accordance with his lights. He believed that suffering was the just punishment of all who did not agree in the smallest detail with the laws as set down by the Church, for they were weakening the foundations of that great Body of which he was the Head. He worshipped the Church, its ceremonies and its doctrines; and as the teaching of Christ was hidden far beneath the many wrappings of creeds and dogmas about that Body, he had lost sight of it; therefore he had no more compunction in commanding that the utmost brutality he administered to those who threatened that Body than we have in attacking the virus of diseases which threaten the human body.

The Church was all-important; and he left the Papacy stronger than he found it.

His character is displayed by his actions with regard to Frederick II of Sicily. When Emperor Henry VI died leaving little Frederick, who was only four years old, as King of Sicily, Constance, the mother of Frederick, in terror of those who she knew would seek to snatch the throne from a helpless child, called upon Innocent to help her. Innocent was benign; he was sorry for this poor woman and her little child. He therefore took them under the apostolic mantle and looked after their interests. It was a kindly action; but Innocent, conscious of the need to strengthen the Papacy, could not resist adding common sense to kindness. Therefore, while being kind to Constance and her baby son, he did not omit to increase Papal influence in Sicily; and later, he acknowledged Frederick as King only when greater privileges were surrendered to the Papacy. Yet when Constance died and left her son in the Pope's charge, he cared for him assiduously and arranged a marriage for him; and there is no doubt that the boy, alone in a harsh world, had a great deal for which to thank Innocent. But Innocent, being Innocent, did not omit to demand his dues.

It was during his reign as Pope that the Mendicant Orders, founded by St Francis and St Dominic, were brought into being. Here were two Orders built on the best possible foundation, two communities which would live humbly and go among the people to preach the gospel even as had Christ Himself.

It is a pity that both have been tainted by their association with the Inquisition.

The Franciscans, after the death of their founder, forgot the original intention, accumulated great wealth and instituted ceremonies calculated to appeal to sensationalism rather than piety. With the Dominicans they went among the people to seek out heresy and stamp on it. The Franciscans however were simpler men than the Dominicans who were noted for their intellectual powers and theological education. It was the Dominicans who set out to teach men how to think; and their name has been more closely associated with the Inquisition than that of the followers of St Francis.

In fact when one visualizes the horror of that monstrous institution pictures of the Dominicans must inevitably rise to the mind. When one thinks of that knock on a door in the night which called men and women from their beds to the prisons of the Inquisition, when one recalls the dank gloom of the torture chambers, one sees always in the background of these piteous scenes the sinister cowled figures – the followers of Domingo de Guzman whom Gregory IX canonized in the year 1234, and who then became St Dominic.

St Dominic, son of Felix Guzman and Joanna of Aza, belonged to a noble Spanish House; and it appears, was the most pious member of a pious family, for his brothers, Antonio and Manes, were both of a highly religious nature. Indeed, there was a saintliness about these brothers which almost matched that of St Dominic particularly in the case of Antonio who, after he had given his fortune to the poor, became a secular priest and spent his life working in a hospital.

There can be no doubt that the Guzman brothers wished to follow Christ's teaching.

Their uncle was Gumiel d'Izan, an archpriest; so it is not surprising that the family of brothers were imbued with religious instincts.

Dominic was as saintly in his habits as was Antonio. In the year 1184, when at the age of fourteen he was put to study in Palencia University, he distinguished himself by going among the poor and relieving their misery as far as was in his power. There is a story that he sold his books that he might have money to buy food for them; and Bartholomew of Trent, who was his contemporary, assures us that on two occasions he would have sold himself into slavery in order to raise ransom money demanded by the Moors for certain men whom they had taken captive. This may well be apocryphal, but at the same time it seems certain, from these remarks of one who lived close to him, that St Dominic was noted for his unselfish and saintly way of life.

It is to be regretted that he was called to help in the extirpation of the heretic; and it seems incredible that a man, such as St Dominic is presented to be, could be capable of giving himself so wholeheartedly – as he undoubtedly did – to this cruel task.

But Dominic was at heart a reformer concerned with reforming the masses, and like most of his kind lacked the gentleness, the concern for the feeling and comfort of *individuals*, which is often felt and shown by people who are otherwise less admirable.

His friend Francesco Bernardone, the son of a rich merchant of Assisi, was of a different nature. It is difficult to imagine that St Francis dedicated himself so fiercely to the destruction of his fellow men. The characters of the two saints must have been entirely opposite, although they both, at one time in their lives, appeared to be setting out on a similar path.

Dominic's life is dramatic, for he might so well have spent it in obscurity and be no better known than his brothers, Antonio and Manes, but for the fact that he happened to be in France at that time when Innocent had despatched his Legates to preach the wisdom of bringing back the rebellious Albigenses to the Church.

When Dominic was a student his piety had been observed, and he had been called by Don Martin de Bazan, who was the Bishop of Osma, to the Cathedral Chapter; and when Don Diego d'Azevedo became Bishop he made Dominic the Superior of the Chapter. He was know as the Prior, and there followed nine pleasant years of meditation and great sanctity in the Chapter House.

Here it seemed that he would remain for the rest of his life, but events forced him out of his obscurity. This happened when the Bishop was sent on an embassy by Alfonso IX, the King of Castile. Bishop Diego d'Azevedo decided that Dominic should accompany him, and thus it was that the Prior found himself in Toulouse when the discouraged Legates were in that town.

Dominic, surveying the pomp of the Legates, then expressed his belief that if these emissaries of the Pope had come in the manner of Christ, their Master, they might have made a deeper impression on the heretics; and thus in the brain of Dominic was born the idea of founding an Order which should consist of mendicant friars who set out to preach the gospel in the steps of the Master.

This was indeed a worthy idea, and characteristic of St Dominic at this stage; but he was by nature a reformer, a military general, rather than a loving Shepherd.

The embassy on which he and Diego d'Azevedo had set out was to arrange a marriage for Ferdinand, the son of Alfonso IX, King of Castile, and having successfully accomplished this they were sent on a second journey to bring home the bride. The young Princess however died before they could set out on the return journey and, finding themselves far from home, with no duties to perform, the two priests decided that they would visit the Pope.

Their travels had roused fervent desires within them both; they had seen the heretic in Southern France, and they both longed to go into the world and bring back to the true fold those who were straying.

Innocent was unimpressed; he told them that if they wished to work among the heretics, they could join the Cistercians, whom he had sent to France, and work with them. There was nothing the two could do but obey, and so fervent were they that they did prevail upon the Cistercians to give up their love of luxury and live simply.

Indefatigably did Dominic work; he was the true fanatic. With the assassination of Castelnau and the war against the Albigenses, he became a close friend of Simon de Montfort.

Catholic historians, eager to exonerate their Saint from the charge of cruelty, tell us that we are wrong to label him 'The First Inquisitor'. They are at pains to insist that the charges of cruelty and fierce zealotry are unfounded. He was a good man, they insist; and we must agree that in part he was a good man. Oh, but that blind spot, that assumption that 'I am right, and you who do not agree with me are wrong' – how often has that tainted the character of the best of men!

Dominic was obviously a man who *wished* to do good. He was sincere; no one doubts it. He lived a life of piety and saintliness in his Chapter House. But at the same time this man was a friend of Simon de Montfort and was present during the siege of many towns; he must have witnessed hideous cruelty, approving of this because the men, women and the children who were being tortured, tormented and subjected to hideous and humiliating death were only heretics, whom his God (made in his own image) would commit to eternal damnation because they had failed to believe in the dogma accepted by the Roman Catholic Church. As if these people could really believe at will! The arrogance in assuming that his particular sect and that only had the right answer cannot surely be reconciled with the humility which must be an essential part of saintliness. What is the use of walking about the Earth, in a plain robe, with bare feet and in all humility, when the mind is as arrogant as all those possessed by religious persecutors must be.

St Dominic, like most of us, had a character which was partly good and partly bad. There is no doubt though that he *wished* to be good; and because he wished to be good his blindness in dealing with heretics must perhaps be forgiven. But what a pity that he did not continue in his Chapter House, living his quiet life in the manner of Brother Antonio; what a pity that, wherever his name and that of his foundation is mentioned, the first feelings they arouse in the minds of all those who do not see the Inquisition as a 'much maligned institution' is one of horror and revulsion.

In an apology for the Inquisition of the *Catholic Encyclopedia*, Joseph Blözer, writing round about the year 1909, tries to explain why the Inquisition arouses such horror among people of this century. It is worth quoting.

'Moderns experience difficulty in understanding this institution because they have to some extent lost sight of two facts. On the one hand they have ceased to grasp religious belief as something objective, as the gift of God, and therefore outside the realm of private judgements; on the other hand they no longer see in the Church a society perfect and sovereign based substantially on a pure and authentic revelation whose first and most important duty must naturally be to retain unsullied this original deposit of faith.'

All one can say to this is: What a happy state of affairs that 'moderns' cannot condone this institution. May the moderns of the centuries to come regard it in the disgust with which it is largely regarded today – and more also.

It was in 1214 when St Dominic founded his Order. In this he was helped by Foulques, the Bishop of Toulouse, who made him Chaplain of Fanjeaux that he might have some property and funds for the use of the Order. From the first the main aim of the Dominicans was the extirpation of heresy.

Thereafter St Dominic travelled widely and established his monasteries in various countries, making his way to those districts which were most infected by heresy.

There are many stories of his virtues. We hear that when terrible pillage was being carried out in the streets of St Béziers, St Dominic walked bravely among the soldiers, holding his cross high, imploring them to show mercy to the women and the children and those who were old or sick. We are told that in his role of First Inquisitor he was merciful and forbearing. Yet he spent a great deal of time with the armies which were waging such hideous war against the Albigenses; the victory for the Church at Muret is said to have been a miracle due to his intercession, for, while the battle was in progress he had knelt in prayer before the altar at the Church of St Jacques, and the battle had gone against the heretics.

All the stories of his virtues, all the tales of his saintliness cannot compensate for the zeal he displayed in hounding the heretic. He, St Dominic will be remembered as the first Inquisitor, the founder of the Dominicans, that order which was responsible for the development of the Inquisition, and the coming to power of men such as Tomás de Torquemada.

St Dominic died in the year 1221. Pope Innocent III was already dead and had been followed in 1216 'most reluctantly' by Honorius III, who was very old. He was eager, even as his predecessor had been, that heresy should be stamped out, but he lacked the vigour of Innocent, and it was not until the election of Ugolino, Count of Segni, as Gregory IX, that the Inquisition was firmly established.

Gregory was also a very old man at the time of his election; this was probably why he was elected. He was about eighty (there is some doubt as to his actual birth date and he may even have been eighty-two). He had been Papal chaplain, Archpriest of St Peter's and Cardinal of Sant' Eustachio under Innocent III, and was awarded more honours under Honorius III.

Honorius died in March 1227, and when the Cardinals assembled to elect a new Pope they agreed to do this by compromise, choosing three among them to decide who should follow Honorius to the Papal throne. One of the three was Conrad of Urach, and he was chosen; but Conrad, fearing that it might be thought that he had been responsible for his own election, refused the honour. A conclave was then held with the result that Ugolino, Count of Segni, was elected. So old was he that it seemed certain there would be another election before long; but Ugolino surprised everybody by living until he was almost a hundred, and because of his actions he has become the most notorious Pope of the Middle Ages.

When he took the tiara with the usual reluctance and became Gregory IX, he followed in the footsteps of Innocent III inasmuch as he was a fervent persecutor of heretics and greatly desirous of winning the Holy Land from the Saracen.

He had been in office only a few days when he began haranguing the Emperor Frederick II to set out on a crusade to the Holy Land. He believed that Frederick was the man in Europe best equipped to go into battle against the Infidel; but Frederick, in spite of a vow he had made, was in no hurry to embark.

He found however that the new Pope was less inclined to leniency than Honorius III had been, and Gregory very quickly made it plain that, unless Frederick was ready to set out at once on the Holy campaign, he might discover something to his disadvantage.

Innocent III had empowered the Papacy to such an extent that Frederick realized he would be wise to act, and he forthwith set out in the September of 1227 for the Holy Land; but after three days he made an excuse to return to his dominions: one of his companions, the Landgrave of Thuringia, had contracted an illness which, Frederick declared, might prove fatal if he continued the journey.

Furious, Gregory excommunicated the Emperor. This gives an indication of the fierce fanaticism of Gregory, the determination to force those in his power to serve his God in the way he thought best, ignoring their desires and their beliefs.

He immediately turned his attention to the extirpation of

34

heretics and was delighted with the work which was being done by those two mendicant orders founded by Francesco Bernardone and Domingo de Guzman. These two men had been great friends of his and Gregory had, before his election, often delighted to go among their followers, simply garbed as they were, and discuss with them matters of theology and the great need to wipe heresy from the face of the Earth. Gregory canonized Francesco, who became St Francis of Assisi on 16th July, 1228; and the same honour was accorded to Domingo on 13th July, 1234.

He showered honours on these two orders – the Franciscans and the Dominicans – and quickly realized what good work they were doing in the fight against heresy.

In 1229, Gregory called an ecclesiastical council in Toulouse. The decree which came out of this was that heretics and their abettors (having been discovered by the Inquisitors) should be handed to the magistrates and nobles – in other words the secular arm – for punishment. This was, in what were called 'cases of obstinacy', death by burning at the stake. A death which, it is pointed out by apologists for the Inquisition, was recognized as the just punishment of traitors to the state; traitors to the rulers of the country, so goes on the apology, were guilty of *lèse-majestè* and therefore were considered deserving of this horrible death; how much greater then was the sin of treason against God! Therefore it is argued these death sentences grew out of a love of justice, not cruelty towards mankind!

While Gregory was absent from Rome during the years 1228 to 1231, heretics in that city made the most of his absence and, as a result, on his return he found many people questioning the dogma of the Church. He thereupon set about cleansing his own city; arrests were numerous; and those who insisted on their right to their own opinions were publicly burned that all might take warning; those who were prepared to admit their fault were imprisoned, and monasteries – Monte Cassino, Cava and Benedictine – were full of those who must be 'persuaded' to confess to their evil ways or, having repented, expiate that greatest of all sins – falling into heresy.

The monster was about to grow to maturity; in the previous

centuries he had been but a sickly infant compared with what he was now to become.

Excommunication was threatened to those who concealed, defended or in any way abetted heretics; and the threat lay over all those lands under Papal jurisdiction like a threatening cloud which would, at the smallest false step or through ill-luck, break about the heads of its victims.

It might be wondered why people should have so feared excommunication; but when the meaning of the Ban of the Church is understood it is easy to see why it should have been so dreaded. Those who were excommunicated from the Church could hold no office; they had no rights as citizens; if they were ill or in any trouble no one was allowed to help them. They were completely shut off from human charity. Perhaps one of the most evil aspects of the ban was that anyone who showed charity to an excommunicated person became himself a candidate for excommunication.

It is extraordinary that these men calling themselves Christians could have set up laws which were in so many ways the complete reverse of Christian teaching.

'. . . faith, hope and charity, these three, and the greatest of these is charity.'

What did these men think when they read words such as those? The fact is that they ignored them. They had rejected the simple faith, and had set up their own in its place. The only resemblance to Christianity it appeared to have was in the name.

At this time the Spanish Dominican, Raymond of Peñaforte, had come to the notice of the Pope. Raymond, canonized by Clement VIII in 1601, was an ardent believer in the duty of all Catholics to persecute the heretic.

He was born at Villafranca de Bernadis near Barcelona and had studied canon law so assiduously that he had become a professor in this subject. After some years he left Spain for Italy, while occupying a chair of canon law in the university of Bologna, he wrote a treatise dealing with ecclesiastical legislation which attracted a great deal of attention.

He had listened to the preaching of the Dominicans, had

become interested in the order and eventually returned to Spain to become a Dominican. There he was so concerned with the conversion of Jews and Moslems to the Christian Faith that he set up institutes where oriental languages were studied by those who would go among Jews and Infidels and preach the gospel.

Such a man was certain to draw attention to himself, and in the year 1230 Gregory summoned him to Rome. So impressed was the Pope by the writings of this man (Raymond had at this time produced his *Summa Casuum*) that he gave him the task of reconstructing the canons of the Church.

This brought to Raymond the chance he had been waiting for, and when his work was completed Gregory gave orders that it, and it alone, should be considered the true authority and none other should be used in schools.

Thus Raymond Peñaforte takes his place among the personalities who were concerned with the building of the Inquisition, and it is for this work that he is remembered in history.

It was in the year 1232 that Gregory established the Inquisition. In his Bull he declared that all heretics should suffer excommunication. Those who were condemned should not suffer their punishment at the hands of the Church but be handed over to the secular arm that sentence might be given and carried out by that body. The punishment for the unrepentant was burning at the stake; and even those who, having been found guilty of heresy, wished to repent, must suffer punishment, though not that of death. They should be condemned to perpetual imprisonment. All those who helped heretics in any way should suffer excommunication; and any who showed friendship for the excommunicated should themselves suffer excommunication. Those who were in such circumstances excommunicated would be given one year in which to prove they were not tainted with heresy; if they failed to do this, then they would fall into the hands of the Inquisition. Anyone discovered giving an excommunicated person Christian burial, should immediately be excommunicated and he should suffer under the ban until he took the offending corpse from its place of burial and arranged that, ever after, no one of the faith should be buried therein.

Any persons, knowing that heresy existed, were bound in duty to the Church to inform on this; failing to do so they would incur excommunication, and suspicion of being themselves involved in heresy.

Children of heretics, and of any who were found guilty of helping heretics, should lose their right to any public office, to the second generation.

These were the rules; in the name of Christianity had been established the Inquisition which was to bring misery and death to tens of thousands in the centuries to come.

The Inquisitors, those cowled figures, who were to strike terror wherever they appeared, were to be the Dominicans and the Franciscans – those two orders which had been founded by two saintly men, who had become imbued with the desire to serve Christ: St Dominic and St Francis.

It seems ironical that these monks should have been the first of the Inquisitors. But more ironical still is the appalling truth that the Inquisition itself was set up in the name of Jesus Christ.

CHAPTER THREE

THE INQUISITION IN SOME EUROPEAN COUNTRIES

It is interesting to follow the spread of the Inquisition in various European countries, and to see how it was largely rejected, mostly through popular feeling.

Conrad of Marburg made a great effort to establish it in Germany.

He was a very earnest persecutor of heretics; and certainly he had his worries in a land such a Germany, where there were men who were interested in new ideas and ready to brave dangers to express and discuss them.

By some historians Conrad is said to have belonged to a monastic order (Henke says a Franciscan, Hausrath a Dominican), but J. P. Kirsch in the *Catholic Encyclopedia* writes that 'according to the Thuringian court chaplain Bethold and Caesarius Heisterback he was probably a secular priest.'

In any case none could have been more ardent in his pursuit of the heretic and the various sects which were, in the first half of the thirteenth century, becoming very numerous in Germany.

Conrad's determination to fight heretics, and his manner of preaching, soon attracted the attention of Ludwig, the Landgrave of Thuringia.

The Landgravine was a very pious lady, Elizabeth, who was the daughter of André II of Hungary. It had in the first place been arranged that Elizabeth should marry the eldest son of Landgrave Hermann I of Thuringia, and she had accordingly been brought from Hungary to the Court of Thuringia at a very early age. This Court was reputed to be licentious, and it was said that the little girl was jeered at for her piety. Hermann however died and, like so many princesses in similar circumstances, little Elizabeth was passed on to Ludwig who was the second son. She was only fourteen at the time of the marriage, Ludwig being twenty-one; and she was very fortunate in having a husband who was almost as strongly attracted by piety as she was herself.

It was to the Court of Thuringia that Conrad was called because Elizabeth's confessor had left her; and, considering all he knew of Conrad, Ludwig believed that Elizabeth could not have a better mentor than the saintly but energetic man.

Conrad was in his element, for Elizabeth was not only eager to be corrected, she wished to be corrected with harshness so that she might subdue her body and live the life of a saint. We are told that even Conrad had to forbid her to punish herself too drastically, though often corporal punishment was applied.

To us today there appear to be so many ways of doing good in the world and living a really Christian life that it seems a somewhat pointless gesture to flagellate the body and torment

39

it with hair-shirt and privation. We might even ask if these self-inflicted tortures are not the result of pride – a pride in the ability to suffer. Is, somewhere in the mind, the thought: 'See how good I am! See how I inflict torment on my body!' We might ask: 'But how, in torturing your flesh, are you carrying out the commands of Christ to love your neighbour? Of what use is this to your fellow men? That they may follow your example and torture *their* bodies? But for what purpose?' But perhaps it is simpler to mortify the flesh in this heroic manner than to lead a simple Christian life which asks too much when it demands forgetfulness of self.

However, this was Elizabeth's way of living a saintly life and there can be no doubt of her sincerity.

In 1227, six years after her marriage, Ludwig who had gone off on a Crusade with the Emperor Frederick II died at Otranto. Elizabeth's third child had just been born and, being heart-broken when she heard the news, she declared that her life was over; but she became more pious than ever. When she died four years later there was great talk of her saintliness; and miracles, it was said, were performed on her grave.

Conrad, who had known her so well, and could vouch for the truth of the life she had led, was asked to bear witness as to her saintliness; and in 1235, four years after her death, she was canonized.

Meanwhile heresy had spread rapidly throughout Germany and Conrad received orders from Rome. He was to be the Papal Inquisitor of Germany.

This task delighted Conrad; he now put all his vigour into smelling out heretics, and this he set about doing with the help of a Dominican, Conrad Dorso, a Franciscan, Gerhard Lutzelkolb, and his servant John. These last were not learned men, but they had enough fanaticism to make up for that; and there began a reign of terror. A careless word, a look, conversation with one whose views might smack of heresy, were enough to bring a man before the Papal Inquisitor; and once there is was very difficult for him to escape.

Conrad believed that the more violent the persecution, the more easily could he destroy heresy. German though he was, he did not understand the Germans. They were a quiet people but

40

a determined one. They watched men whom they had loved and respected being burned at the stake; they said little, but a strong determination was forming in their hearts; and in spite of the seeming quiet there was unrest in Germany, and the most hated of men was the Papal Inquisitor.

Conrad either was unaware of this unrest or did not care. He continued on his way and, when one of the most powerful and influential noblemen of the land acted carelessly, he did not hesitate to summon him to appear before the tribunal. This was the Count of Sayn.

The Count was very angry and demanded a fair hearing. Conrad was soon to appreciate not only the temper of the German people but that he was far from Rome. A fair trial was demanded for the Count and he got it, with the result that the charge of heresy broke down. The Count was released; and the spirits of the Germans rose accordingly.

Conrad, however, continued as violent as ever in his persecution, but the people had taken courage from the affair of Count Sayn and, one evening when Conrad and Lutzekolb were returning to Marburg, they were set upon by a group of men who were determined to take revenge for all the misery Conrad had brought to their friends and relations.

After that encounter Conrad and his henchmen were left lying dead on the ground.

In Rome Gregory might rage; he might determine to have the murderers of his faithful servants punished with the utmost severity; but whatever he did, he had received an indication of what Germany's answer to the Inquisition was likely to be; and all through the thirteenth century, although the Holy Office was still represented in Germany, after the murder of Conrad it did not establish itself with any real firmness.

Urban V, a Pope noted for his ascetic nature, who occupied the Papal throne from 1362 to 1370, dissatisfied with the state of affairs in Germany, despatched two Dominican monks to the country with threats to the prelates there of excommunication if they did not give full support to his emissaries; nor was the Emperor Charles IV spared the Pope's reproaches.

There had now arisen several new sects among whom were the Flagellants from Italy. They believed that the end of the world was in sight and that God would forgive their sins and those of the world if they scourged their bodies.

Charles IV, afraid, as so many had been before and would be henceforward, of the dreaded threat of excommunication, received the newly-appointed Inquisitors with honours; he sanctioned the censorship of literature, which censorship soon began to have its effect: the dissenters began to move out of Germany to other parts of Europe.

Kerlinger, the new chief Inquisitor, went to work with an enthusiasm and harshness common to his kind, and there was great suffering in certain towns; but the bishops, who believed that they had been slighted by the coming of the Inquisitors, were not always inclined to work with them; and on the death of Urban V and the election of Gregory XI, the bishops informed the new Pope that inquisitorial conduct had not always been exemplary.

Gregory ordered an investigation, and when the bishops' statements were proved to be correct, the Pope gave the bishops new powers over the rival Inquisitors. This lack of unity was a further blow to the Inquisition.

With the coming of the fifteenth and sixteenth centuries the Inquisition suffered further setbacks. Germany during those centuries brought forth men of great intellectual power, such as Johann Wessel, and most important of all, Martin Luther.

Wessel who lived from 1420 to 1489, was a great reformer, a John the Baptist of the Reformation; he was a teacher and known to thousands as *Lux Mundi*.

There was Desiderius Erasmus, born in Rotterdam in 1466, who was to exercise a tremendous influence over European thought, and particularly in Germany, for it was often said that Erasmus was the man to lay the egg, although Martin Luther was the one to hatch it.

Erasmus started life under the cloud of illegitimacy, but he soon overcame this and during a six years' sojourn in a monastery he studied the manners and habits of monks and was not inclined to admire what he saw. He then began that series of writings which were to be the prelude to the Reformation; and books such as *Praise of Folly* must have caused a great deal of apprehension in Inquisitorial circles. He died in 1536, ten years

42

before the death of Martin Luther. In his sixty-nine years he had left a significant mark on the world.

Then came the great reformer himself. He was born in the year 1483 at Eisleben, Prussian Saxony. His childhood was one of great hardship, for he was born into poverty; but from earliest days he displayed great intellectual powers and was put to the study of law. However he was more interested in theology, and it was when he entered an Augustine order that he made the discovery that men could not expect salvation merely by the singing of masses.

His views attracted the attention of the Elector of Saxony who gave him an appointment at Wittenburg. Here he might have continued in moderate obscurity had not John Tetzel, a Dominican, arrived from Rome with indulgences for sale, the object being to raise money to rebuild St Peter's which, dating back to 306, was falling into decay. Luther's anger at the selling of indulgences was aroused and there followed the famous gesture of denunciation.

Retaliation came from Rome: Luther's writings were to be burned; he himself was summoned to the Diet of Worms. But the Inquisition which had grown feeble with the years was powerless against him.

He continued with his writings, and when he died in 1546 he had created a powerful rival to the Catholic Church; and it had become clear that in Germany the Holy Office was no longer effective, no longer to be feared.

In France the Inquisition began with a firmer start. The Albigensian war had made the way easy. Yet when Guillem Arnaud came with his pioneering spirit and the might of Gregory I behind him, his cruelty aroused such anger among the people that he and his assistants received the same treatment as Conrad and Lutzelkolb, and were murdered.

However the Pope was determined that the Inquisition should be established in France; and there began that long struggle between the Kings of France and the Popes for the right to stand supreme in that country.

This came to its climax when Philip IV, known as the Fair, ascended the throne in 1285. No sooner had he done so than he announced his determination to prevent the spread of the Church's power in his dominions; moreover he meant to curtail that which already existed. This attitude of Philip's resulted in the famous struggle between himself and Boniface VIII. Philip had, before the election of Boniface, already taken from the clergy certain judicial powers and placed them in civic hands; and Boniface was, even on his accession, in a weak position because in the great family of Colonnas he had enemies in his own city; for this reason he had no intention at this stage of raising an issue with the King of France whose friendship he could not afford to lose.

But in the year 1296, when Philip the Fair was at war with the English and the Flemish, he imposed fresh taxes on the clergy, who took their grievances to Boniface. Boniface, two years in office, immediately came to the rescue of his suffering prelates, and declared that clerics could not pay further taxes without the consent of the Pope; at the same time he implied that, although Kings and Emperors might be the rulers of their lands, there was one who was above them all and to whom they owed allegiance: the Holy Father himself. Failure to recognize this vital fact, Boniface pointed out, could result in excommunication.

Philip was furious; but he was at war, and he decided to wait awhile before taking action. However he commanded his merchants to cease the export of gold and silver which had been previously sent to Rome; and thus a large source of revenue was prevented from entering that city.

Boniface now began to realize that he had a formidable enemy in the King of France; and weakly he issued a Bull which allowed the French King to collect taxes from his clergy provided there was great need to do so. To show his appreciation, Philip, who had previously limited the power of the Inquisitors in France, now relaxed his veto.

However, when there was a dispute between Philip and the Bishop of Narbonne on account of certain monies which each declared should have come to him, the Pope took the side of the Bishop against the King, and Boniface wrote sternly to Philip: 'If, my son, you tolerate such actions against the Churches of your kingdom, you should tremble lest God, author of judgments and King of Kings, take vengeance on you.'

Philip's fury at such words was great; but the Pope did not content himself with words only; he sent to Paris as his Legate the newly appointed Bishop of Pamiers, Bernard de Saisset.

This was an unhappy move because Bernard was a Languedocian and a natural enemy of Philip; the domination of the north over the south of France, which had followed the war against the Albigenses, rankled in the heart of Bernard; moreover he was a descendant of the Counts of Toulouse, and no sooner had he arrived in Paris than he became rather abusive and even went so far as to declare that Philip could only be said to descend from Charlemagne through an illegitimate line.

The incensed Philip summoned Bernard to Senlis to answer a charge of plotting against the King and State; Philip's two faithful servants, Pierre Flotte who was his Chancellor, and Guillaume de Nogaret who was judge-major at Beaucaire, had always been determined to withstand the domination of the Church. As a result of the investigation at Senlis Bernard was arrested, and Philip despatched the Chancellor and the judge-major to Rome with a letter to Boniface in which he asked that Bernard be divested of his orders and privilege.

Boniface's answer was to ask that Bernard be sent back to him. His note was somewhat threatening, for he warned Philip of the displeasure of God if the possessions of the Bishop of Pamiers were seized by the King of France. He pointed out to the King's emissaries that the power of the Pope was spiritual, and that it embraced the temporal power of kings, which was included in the spiritual power of the Holy See.

Pierre Flotte retorted boldly that this might be so, but the power of the Pope over events in France was merely nominal; whereas in France the power of the King was very real indeed.

This angered Boniface who was given to violent outbreaks of temper; whereupon he demanded that Philip the Fair acknowledge the all-embracing power of the Holy See.

The result was an exchange of acrimonious notes; one of which coming from the Pope, the King burned ceremoniously before a crowd of his subjects in Paris. Afterwards Philip called to the capital an assembly which was to consist of the most important people from all over the country – two or three men representing each of the cities. They met in Notre-Dame, and this meeting has often been called the first States General of France.

Philip then proclaimed his desire to reform the existing laws between Church and State; and, as a result of the meeting, letters were sent to Rome deploring the Pope's interference in temporal matters.

Although most of the country stood for the King there was opposition from forty-five Bishops who insisted that both temporal and spiritual power lay in the hands of the Church; and that temporal power was held by kings only with the consent of the sovereign of them all: the Pope. All people, they declared, were subject to the Pontiff; moreover only those who believed this could enjoy salvation.

Philip's retort was to put the Bishops under restraint and to forbid them to leave his kingdom; while Boniface ordered them to come at once to Rome.

The conflict between King and Pope was drawing to its climax. Philip held a Council at the Louvre during which one of his most trusted advisers, Guilliaume de Plasian, set forth an accusation against the Pope, and there was a demand that a new Pope should be elected who could be a true Defender of the Faith.

Boniface's reply was that if the King of France did not mend his ways he would have to be chastised and treated as a little boy; and he added that unless the Bishops whom he had commanded to come to Rome were allowed to leave French territory at once, the King of France would be excommunicated.

Philip was a little alarmed at this, for the threat of excommunication had always carried dread with it; he was afraid that his subjects, who had for so many generations blindly obeyed the rules of the Church, might feel it their duty, once the Ban was laid upon their King to desert him. He therefore demanded the support of the churches and universities insomuch that they should make it known that all those who came within their sway should ignore the Pope's orders and obey only their King.

A few refused; among these was the Abbot of Cîteaux and

the Templars. The latter were very soon to pay dearly for this.

The King, feeling that he had the support of his country behind him, sent Guillaume de Nogaret to interview the Pope who was staying at the little town of Anagni where he had been born. News had reached Philip that Boniface had been received by the people of Anagni with the utmost respect and affection; moreover they had, in their eagerness to show their support for the Pope, insulted his enemy by taking the banner of France and dragging the sacred lilies in the dust.

Before going to Anagni, Guillaume de Nogaret sought out the old enemies of Boniface in Rome, the Colonnas, and by paying them handsomely had secured their services.

One of the family, Sciarra Colonna, hated the Pope more than most. He was a harsh man who had been captured by pirates at one time of his life and worked as a galley slave. Had he revealed the fact that he was a Colonna, there would have been no doubt that the corsairs would have asked the Pope to pay a ransom for his freedom; but the proud Colonna, determined to ask no favours of an enemy, preferred to endure the life of a slave for a year before escaping.

Sciarra was only too willing to accompany Nogaret to Anagni; and with their few followers they rode into the town shouting 'Death to Boniface! Long Life to Philip the Fair and the Lilies of France!'

The simple people of that little town were terrified when they heard the shouts for they thought that the armies of France were coming against them. They ran into their houses and barricaded themselves in, forgetting that they had promised to protect the Holy Father. Thus was the Pope left alone to face his enemies.

Sciarra Colonna demanded that he abdicate immediately.

This Boniface refused to do. 'I am betrayed,' he said bravely, 'as Jesus was betrayed. I may die, but I shall die Pope.' He had great dignity in that moment, for he was seventy-five, yet he faced them appearing unafraid, magnificently dressed – he had prepared himself to meet them – in the cloak of St Peter and the crown of Constantine, the cross and the keys in his hands.

The Colonna would have killed him on the spot, and it is said that he actually did strike the Pope across the face with his mailed hand, which must have been very painful for the old man. However, the courage of Boniface persisted and Guillaume de Nogaret, realizing that it would be unwise deliberately to murder the Pope, prevented the Colonna from going farther.

'Caitiff Pope,' we are told he said, 'confess and enjoy the mercy of my sovereign, the King of France, who, though far away, watches over you and defends you through my hands.'

Thereupon the Frenchman took the Pope into custody where he remained for three days; but by that time the townspeople, ashamed of their desertion, gathered together and, assuring themselves that it was not an army which had come against them but only a few foreigners, went in a body to the house in which he was held prisoner and secured his release.

When they brought him out into the streets his plight was pitiful. He was hungry and thirsty, and the kind people of Anagni brought him bread and wine and sustained him, not only with food and drink, but shouts of 'Long Live His Holiness!'

He set out for Rome, and the crowds went with him; but the ordeal through which he had passed had proved too much for him.

He did reach the city but immediately became very ill. Some say that he was overcome by fever; others declare that he fell into such a mad rage that he lost his reason. There is probably no truth in this latter; it may well be a statement circulated by his contemporary enemies and preserved by others who came after. There is no doubt that Boniface was a fanatic, but so were many other people; and there is a distinction between fanaticism and madness. It may be true that he was subject to fits of rage which left him blind to the views of others and stubbornly determined to cling to his own; but this is a common enough human weakness. Boniface was ambitious, cunning and proud; it was unfortunate for him that he had been called upon to do battle with an enemy who was more ambitious, more proud, more cunning – and perhaps infinitely more cruel.

He died in Rome on 11th October, 1303. He had tried to follow in the footsteps of Innocent III who had extended the Papal authority throughout Europe; he had failed to see that since the reign of Innocent, nearly a hundred years before, great changes had come about, and power was passing from the Papacy to the secular rulers. In fighting to retain what had become impossible to hold, he had not only come to his own unfortunate end, but had done nothing to uphold the prestige of the Holy See.

Philip was determined to make the most of the advantage he had secured and when, shortly after the death of Boniface, Benedict XI was elected, he sent his congratulations through Guillaume de Plasian together with an intimation that he would expect the new Pope to profit from the lesson of the old and understand that if he would remain secure he must not forget the power of the King of France.

Benedict did realize the need to placate the most powerful monarch in Europe and immediately lifted the ban of excommunication against the King and the French nobles; however, he did not feel that he could show the same leniency towards Guillaume de Nogaret and those Frenchmen who had actually gone to Anagni and confronted the Pope there in such a manner as to be the indirect cause of his death; nor could he, as Philip wished him to, denounce his predecessor.

In June of 1304 he showed his growing strength by issuing a fresh Bull of excommunication against those who had dared commit a crime against the good memory of Pope Boniface.

Philip received this news in silence, but a month after the launching of that Bull a basket of fresh figs was brought to Benedict; they were so delectable that the Pope ate several of them. Almost immediately afterwards he was dead.

We cannot be sure who poisoned the figs. The name of the Colonnas and Guillaume de Nogaret have been put forward with that of Philip. It seems more likely that Philip – particularly in view of what followed – was the poisoner, for the removal of Benedict was so necessary to his plans and he immediately set about finding a Pope who would give him complete obedience.

This he found in Bertrand de Goth, the Archbishop of Bordeaux who, though known to be no friend of France, was possessed of limitless ambitions; and Philip believed he knew enough of ambition – possessing it in such a degree himself –

that he had no doubt of the lengths to which it could carry a man.

De Goth had little chance of rising above the rank of Archbishop without the help of powerful friends. Philip decided to offer that help – at a price.

He sent for the Archbishop and promised that he would make him Pope if he would grant certain requests of the King. De Goth, overcome with delight at this power which he saw within his grasp, promised the King anything he should ask. Philip smiled, and put forward some of his requests which were simple enough for a Pope to grant. One of Philip's demands was however that the memory of Boniface should be desecrated – which was not a very easy task for the new Pope; the remaining request Philip declared he would not yet divulge, but would demand the granting of it when the time came. Then, keeping the brother and two nephews of de Goth as hostages, he dismissed the Pope-to-be; and a few weeks after his encounter with the King, de Goth became Clement V.

Now Philip knew himself to be the most powerful man in Europe. The only other who might have challenged him was his creature, bound to do his service. One of the first actions of the new Pope under the influence of the King was to move the Papal residence from Rome to Avignon, which was however owned by the Papacy though situated among the dominions of the King of France; this meant that the Pope was under the eye of his master. The period which elapsed before the return of the Papacy to Rome (sixty years) has been called the 'Babylonish captivity'.

It was not long before the King of France made known to Clement the last of his demands. This was the destruction of the Knights Templar.

That he should demand this came as a shock to the Pope, for it was not known that Philip had felt towards them any particular rancour. It was true that they had not supported him against Boniface, but this was an extremely severe punishment for such a small affront.

Philip had other reasons. He needed money, and the Templars were very wealthy. Philip had always been friendly towards this group and had borrowed money from them; but during the year 1306 there had been riots in Paris and it had been necessary for the King to take shelter. This had been offered him in the Temple Palace, the stronghold of the Templars, and while he was in hiding there Philip had discovered the immense value of the treasures which were in the possession of this Order.

Philip was now in great need of money. His wars had impoverished his coffers and he saw a way of replenishing them. He was determined to have the wealth of the Templars.

The Order of the Knights Templar (which had been started, it will be remembered, by nine knights who had made it their duty to conduct pilgrims through the Holy Land, and had become known as the Templars because Baldwin II of Jerusalem had granted them a residence in his palace built on the site of the Temple of Solomon) had changed a great deal since its inception. Founded in 1119 it had grown rapidly; before the end of the twelfth century it had acquired land and wealth all over the Christian world; by the end of the thirteenth century the order had multiplied and become more affluent.

As was probably true regarding most such orders, the original intention was lost – as instance the Franciscans and Dominicans – and with the passing of the years what was intended to be a virtuous and self-sacrificing life became one of luxury and acquisitiveness.

However, now that the Templars had become very rich indeed Philip was bent on acquiring those riches; and Pope Clement, who knew who was his master, could do nothing but acquiesce in view of the promise he made to the King as the price of his election.

Consequently, Jacques de Molai, Grand Master of the Templars, a nobleman of Burgundy who was at the time living in Cyprus, was summoned to Paris by the Pope as well as by the King.

No hint was immediately given of the King's intention, Philip explaining to de Molai that he wished to discuss a new crusade with him. While de Molai was in Paris Philip arranged for the spreading of rumours concerning the evil manner of living into which the Templars were reputed to have fallen. True to his character he gave no hint that he had even heard the rumours, and de Molai imagined himself to be basking in royal favour since he was godfather to one of the King's children and played an important part at the funeral of another member of the royal family.

Philip cunningly allowed some time to pass; then he summoned Clement to meet him at Poitiers; there they discussed the disturbing rumours, and the King declared his desire that there should be an enquiry into them.

It was a simple matter to get the required evidence, and the outcome of the investigation was the arrest of Jacques de Molai and all leading Templars throughout France. The torturing and burning began. Clement might have been ashamed of this treatment of men who, even if they had been guilty of acquiring riches and loving luxury, were certainly innocent of the ridiculous charges brought against them, and in any case had never shown themselves to be enemies of the Holy See.

De Molai and two companions, both high in the Order, were burned to death on 11th March, 1314, in Ile de la Cité where the Place Dauphine was later to stand. They had been hideously tortured and under torture had made the required confessions; but later, confronted by the fire, they recanted these confessions, and before he died the Grand Master declared that woe would come to those who had condemned the Templars without a cause. 'God,' he said, 'will avenge our deaths.'

This gave rise to a rumour that de Molai had cursed those who had been responsible for the terrible tragedy which had befallen the Templars and, because the Pope died in April, a month after the Grand Master had perished at the stake, and Philip only eight months later in November, their deaths gave weight to the rumour.

Philip had received the wealth of the Templars; more important still, he had established for ever in France the power of the Kings over the Papacy.

In 1334 Philip VI allowed the Inquisitors to continue in their privileges, providing they understood that all their power came to them through the crown. The strength of the French monarchy had relegated the Inquisition to that of an organization to be employed when the State needed it, as in the case of the Templars.

That is not to say that hideous persecution was no longer practised in France. In the reign of François Premier the culmination of these horrors was in the notorious massacre of the Vaudois; but even before this melancholy event, those who diverged from the views of the Catholic Church were very severely dealt with; and between November 1534 and May 1535 twenty-four people were burned alive in Paris and many others were sentenced to slightly less terrible fates. The methods used in France were similar to those already being employed by the Inquisition in Spain; victims were chained to planks which were lowered into fires, then raised and lowered again; this was continued until the agonized sufferer became completely unconscious and so afforded little satisfaction to the bestial observers.

François however was no moralist, and his cruelty was a matter of policy; and there were times when he seemed to repent of that cruelty, with the result that persecution was sporadic. His action against the Vaudois will always be recalled with particular disgust.

The Vaudois (or the Waldenses) had settled in the valleys between the Alps and the Juras; and in Dauphiné, Provence and the valleys of the Piedmontese Alps they lived peaceably – quiet people, farmers and shepherds who asked nothing but to be left alone to work and follow their own religion.

Lutherism had spread to their neighbourhood, and this seemed to them a faith of great possibilities.

Pope Paul III, calling François' attention to these people, declared them to be a danger to the Catholic world, and demanded that they should be treated as heretics. As a result many of them were arrested and, on a March day in 1536, thirteen of them were burned alive.

Guillaume du Bellay was sent by François to ascertain what manner of people were these Vaudois whom the Pope was so eager to destroy, and his report disclosed them to be hard-working conscientious and good neighbours to one another; they did not of course conform to the laws of the Church.

François then ordered that any of the Vaudois who, during the following three months, adjured his religion and accepted that of the Orthodox Church should be forgiven past sins.

The result of this edict was that the Vaudois drew up a manifesto, which explained fully their beliefs, and sent the documents to the King and two Bishops, John Durandi, Bishop of Cavaillon, and Cardinal Sadolet, Bishop of Capentras. The latter discussed their beliefs with them, telling them how they must conform; but the sturdy Vaudois pointed out that it was impossible for them to declare their belief in things in which they could not believe.

After this, there followed a period of peace for these persecuted people, the reason being that François was at that time concerned with winning the friendship of the German Protestants; but later, when that need no longer existed, a certain Jean de Maynier, Baron d'Oppède, a cruel and bigoted man of power in Rome, brought accusations, not only of heresy but of a political nature, against the Vaudois. He declared that they were plotting to bring foreign reformers into France with the motive of making Provence an independent state.

This was at the beginning of the year 1545, and François was already becoming exhausted by ill-health brought on by excesses – he was to die two years later – so that when an edict against the Vaudois was presented to him for his signature, he signed it, it is said, without reading it.

The result was the massacre.

Unfortunately for the Vaudois the command of this shameful affair was placed in the cruel hands of Baron d'Oppède.

The Vaudois were without self-defence when the troops descended on them; and these troops were the most brutal of men. The mob followed the army, scenting spoil and loot. None was spared. Women were violated in the most hideous manner the maddened mob and bestial soldiers could devise; they were submitted to every indignity and were continuously raped before their bodies were thrown over cliffs. Men and children were tortured and submitted to lingering or speedy deaths, according to the mood of the tormentors.

Three thousand people were murdered, and two hundred and fifty-five given a mock trial and later executed; between six and seven hundred were condemned to the galleys, and as many children were sold into slavery. Three towns and twenty-two villages were laid waste.

This was the terrible massacre of the Vaudois, those people who had taken refuge together that they might think and act as their consciences bade them.

Two years later, the cynical François on his death-bed recalled this great crime and deeply repented it; he implored his son, Henri Deux, to have an enquiry made into the matter; and in the year 1550, when the massacre was still vividly remembered, Madame de Cental, who had estates in Provence, brought a complaint against the men who had led the assault on her subjects.

D'Oppède, who was accused with Guérin, a man who had been advocate-general in 1545, declared that he had carried out the orders of François Premier and if they condemned him they should condemn Saul who had obeyed God's commands to slay the Amalekites. The powerful Duke of Guise was his friend, and Oppède was therefore released. Not so Guèrin. The King remembered his father's death-bed wish, and there had to be a scapegoat; Guérin supplied the need and was condemned to death.

But even the massacre of the Vaudois pales beside the horror of that of August 1572 – the massacre of the St Bartholomew – when Catholics rose against Huguenots and slaughtered them in their thousands, committing a crime which can never be forgotten.

Persecution there certainly was in France, hideous bigotry, and the foulest murder; but it was not done by the Inquisition.

The *chambre ardente* was instituted, but that was set up by the state. France rejected the Holy Office when Philip IV entered into a struggle with the Papacy, and from that time the Inquisition had no real foothold in France.

The Inquisition started with great strength in Italy. Rome – naturally – and Florence being its strongholds. There was no lack of fervent men to carry on the task of extirpating the heretic; and two of the most well known are the Dominicans. Peter Martyr and Rainerio Sacchoni.

In the early days of the Inquisition the persecuted seemed

more determined to oppose tyranny – perhaps they had greater opportunity of doing so than those who came later – for Peter Martyr met the same fate as had Conrad of Marburg in Germany and Guillem Arnaud in France.

Peter Martyr worked fanatically against heretics in Milan and Florence; and it was in Florence that the people, unable to tolerate his cruelty, rose against him. But the conflict in Italy at this time was bound up in the rivalry between two political parties and was therefore more than merely a struggle to establish the Catholic Faith firmly in Italian territory. These two parties were the Ghibellines and the Guelphs. The Ghibellines wished to uphold the supremacy of the German Emperors over the Italian States, whereas the Guelphs wished to free Italy from German domination, to proclaim the independence of Italy and accept the supremacy of the Holy See.

Peter Martyr was so successful that it was not long before he made the Guelphs triumphant in Florence; this meant that the Inquisition began to flourish freely there.

So zealously did he work however that in the year 1252 he was attacked and murdered by the maddened crowd, according to some accounts at Milan, to others at Como. Thereupon he was nominated the patron saint of the Inquisition.

Rainerio Sacchoni, born at Piacenza, was in his youth a Catharist and even became one of their bishops. For seventeen years he remained with this sect and then, we are told, on hearing the preaching of Peter Martyr he deserted the Catharists and became a Dominican.

Like most converts he was an enthusiast, and when Peter Martyr was murdered he stepped into his shoes and became Inquisitor for Lombardy.

It was not long before he, like Peter, was arousing murderous feelings among the people. They failed to kill him; but so unpopular did he become that it was felt advisable to send him into exile. But before this, Pope Alexander IV had sent forces against two Ghibelline overlords, Uberto da Pallavicino and Eccelin da Romano, and defeated them, with the result that the Inquisition was then set up in the territories of these two lords.

The Inquisition was at the height of its power in Italy at this time; there was of course opposition such as the murder of

Martyr, the exile of Rainerio Sacchoni and the burning of one of the Dominican monasteries in Parma in the year 1279.

Venice refused to accept the Inquisition, and as a result the persecuted began to make their way to that refuge; but Papal authority soon put a stop to this state of affairs, and Venice realized that it would be unwise to hold out against such a power. However, the city was in a position to bargain and although Inquisitors were admitted, the laws of the Inquisition were not incorporated with those of the city and Venice took to herself those goods which were confiscated from heretics. This of course had the result of slackening the desire of the Inquisition for persecutions in that city.

When Charles of Anjou took over Naples he established the Inquisition there, but he made it clear that it was under the control of the head of the State to whom it must look for orders; and this in turn robbed the Papacy of its power.

Yet the Inquisition in Italy was more firmly established and of longer duration than in France; and as late as 1448 there was a crusade against heretics. This however was defeated, and the Waldenses continued to flourish in the mountain areas; and because of the fight put up against the Inquisitors by the people of Italy, because of the frequent flights from those areas which were in the thraldom of the Inquisition, and because of the attitude of such states as Naples and Venice, the Inquisition became considerably weakened throughout the peninsula.

The farther the area from Rome, the more difficult was it to establish the power of the Inquisition, and very little headway was made in those countries situated east of Italy.

Boniface VIII, in 1298, four years after his election to the Papal throne, did his utmost to establish the Inquisition there but without success; and the Dominicans made a further attempt in 1336; but the Catharists were very strong in these countries, and the secular rulers, realizing that these men were good subjects, were very loth to persecute them for heresy.

In 1432 Eugenius IV despatched Giacomo della Marca to Slavonia, for della Marca had distinguished himself as a fiery persecutor of Italian heretics; he had some success but when trouble broke out nearer Rome he was recalled to quell that,

57

and afterwards the futility of sending Inquisitors into Slavonia was realized.

Eventually the Inquisition endeavoured to penetrate into Bohemia, and the first Inquisitors appeared about 1318; but after the treatment accorded to Hus and Jerome the Inquisition was looked upon with great suspicion by the Bohemians; and because they were so far from its centre they were able to prevent its spreading in their country.

Jan Hus was born at Husinetz in South Bohemia in 1369. Having passed through the University of Prague he was ordained and appointed Rector of the University.

He became absorbed in the writings of John Wyclif, Master of Balliol College, Oxford, who had taken upon himself the task of reforming the Church. He had translated the Bible into English and was fearless in his denunication of certain tenets of the Church.

Wyclif became known later as the Morning Star of the Reformation, and he had become greatly admired throughout his University for his attacks on the Mendicant Friars who, while outwardly going among the people in their coarse garments and with a humble air, really possessed great wealth and lived in stately mansions. They were hypocrites, he declared; they flattered the people and granted absolution through the sale of indulgences.

Fortunately for Wyclif he lived in England.

Jan Hus, however, was a very brave man. He translated the works of Wyclif and circulated them.

Innocent VII, hearing what was going on in Prague, fulminated in Rome and ordered the Archbishop Sbinco to take action against Hus. Sbinco obeyed the Pope as best he could, but Prague was far away from Rome and he knew the temper of the Czech people; so although Hus was warned by the Archbishop he continued to state his views from his pulpit where he could be sure of a big and appreciative audience.

By 1408 Gregory XII was on the Papal throne and determined to put a stop to the spread of heresy. He made overtures to the King, Wenceslaus, implying that he was not unaware of the royal tolerance towards the new ideas; and when there were hints of the dreaded excommunication, Wenceslaus stirred himself to action and declared that, since the University of Prague was suspected of permitting heresy in its midst, it must clear itself from that charge.

Hus continued with his preaching, and it was not until 1409, when there was another Pope at the Vatican, Alexander V (Gregory XII's reign had been of only three years' duration), that the Archbishop was ordered to forbid preaching except in cathedrals, or collegiate and parish churches.

Hus, however, no doubt spurred on by the persistence of his hero Wyclif in Oxford, was not to be subdued; he continued to state his views and his supporters grew in number.

They even went so far as to send a protest to the Pope. The Papacy had changed hands again (Alexander V only held office for a year) and the retort of the new Pope, John XXIII, was to excommunicate Hus and all those who agreed with him. This however made little impression, for the supporters of Hus continued loyal.

John XXIII was eager to send forth a new Crusade against the Holy Land and, anxious to raise money for this, he declared that all who supplied funds for the Crusade should be forgiven their sins.

This sale of indulgences was one of the main grievances against the Catholic Church, and was of course later stressed vigorously by Martin Luther; now Hus and Jerome of Prague went into their pulpits and declaimed against such practices.

Furious, John ordered Hus to be imprisoned and his church burned. But John was far away and the Papacy had little influence in Prague. Hus remained free; however, he was prevailed upon to leave Prague; and he retired for a while to the country, where he wrote *Dé ecclesiâ* and prepared his treatise *Dé sex erroribus*.

Afterwards he returned to Prague and the treatise was posted on the walls of his church; heresy was discovered in the treatise and he was invited to appear at the Council of Constance to instruct the Council in his doctrines.

Hus, having lived in comparative security at Prague, felt few qualms about making the journey to the city in south Germany; but on arriving he found he had walked into a trap. They had not asked him to state his doctrine; they had brought him from Prague to try, and condemn him. This they did. He was burned at the stake on the 6th July, 1415.

Jerome of Prague met the same fate a year later.

The people of Bohemia were horrified by these burnings; and when other members of the Husite group were invited, as their leader had been, to appear before the Council, very wisely they refused to leave Prague.

There was little chance therefore of installing the Inquisition with any firmness in a land where there were so many people of fierce independent spirit; and although preachers were sent among the heretics and efforts were made to bring in the Inquisitors, the people of Bohemia kept the Inquisition from their land.

There is one instance of the Inquisition's working in England. This was when Clement V, on instructions from his master, Philip IV of France, issued a proclamation throughout Christendom that there was to be an enquiry into the habits and customs of the Knights Templar.

Action against them had already started in France, and in the year 1309 *plumbea bulla bullatoe* was brought to England and read to the Bishop of London and other members of the clergy in the episcopal hall. In this Bull the Pope informed the Bishop that the Knights Templar had adopted evil habits, and he had been unwilling to believe this until Philip IV of France had brought the matter to his notice and the charge had been proved. He ordered that all Knights Templar in England should be arrested and that a careful examination of these men take place.

Edward II, the English King, who had married the daughter of Philip IV, was ready to obey his father-in-law and the Pope; and forthwith all English Templars were arrested and put in prison at London, York and Lincoln.

The Papal Commissioners visited England to conduct the enquiry but it was very difficult to prove a case against the Templars, who all firmly protested their innocence of the charges brought against them.

Torture in such circumstances was not applied in England,

and without this the Inquisitors realized that they could make little progress. In France they were getting wonderful results; in England there was deadlock.

Clement, with the King of France behind him, thundered forth his instructions that Edward must do his duty, and the weak King forthwith gave orders that the Inquisitors should be allowed to do what they wished with the bodies of the prisoners as that was the ecclesiastical law.

This brought better results; moreover witnesses were found – very unreliable ones – to testify against the Templars; but when the latter were condemned the sentence passed on them was by no means as barbaric as that which their fellows had suffered in France.

They were to be imprisoned for the rest of their lives in monasteries, and their goods were to be confiscated and delivered into the King's hands.

The King, however, who was himself to come to a very unhappy end in Berkeley Castle, was inclined to be lenient with the Templars, and even allowed them a little money with which to support themselves in their prisons: two shillings a day for the Grand Master, and fourpence a day for his Knights.

Edward then distributed their property among his favourites.

The Inquisitors while in England were aware of the hostility of the people. The English did not like the Inquisition. It was surprising how important a strip of water could be; England was divided from Europe by the sea; and public opinion was hostile to the setting up of Inquisitors in their land.

The trial of the Templars was the only occasion when the Inquisition worked in England. That is not to say that there was not persecution in England; but it rarely reached such fanatical heights as on the Continent.

One of the earliest instances of religious persecution occurred in the year 1159 in the reign of Henry II. This was when a very small community, not more than thirty men and women, appeared in England. We do not know who they were because records are sparse and only monks pass down the account to us, and they were, naturally, very prejudiced. Yet the story comes to us that this little community attracted attention to itself because it did not worship God after the manner of the majority.

These people spoke German, so presumably they were refugees from religious persecution on the Continent. It was thought necessary to bring them before the clergy at Oxford, and there it was discovered that their leader was a man named Gerard; he told the Council that he and his followers were Christians but that they denied certain doctrines of the orthodox Church; for instance they did not believe in purgatory, nor that the saints should be invoked when praying for the dead. This seemed to be the extent of the differences but they were judged heretics, and therefore deemed worthy of punishment.

The people who had witnessed their demeanour at the Council of Clergy, and who knew them in their daily life, found them modest and good citizens. But the clergy would not allow them to go unpunished; therefore the King was obliged, in obedience to the Church, to offer judgment and pronounce sentence.

First, all these people were to be branded on their foreheads with hot irons that all might know them for heretics. They were to be stripped to the waist and whipped through the streets of Oxford; and afterwards their clothes were to be cut short and they themselves turned into the fields just as they were. Anyone who dared show a little Christian spirit and a wish to help these people in distress would, of course, be committing a grievous sin against the Church, and in their turn would suffer similar penalties.

It was winter when these poor people, half naked, without food, their wounds bleeding, were turned into the fields to die.

They are said to be the first who suffered as heretics in England; it is sad that they should not have been the last. There is also a terrible story of the persecution of the Jews in England.

Intolerance towards Jews increased rapidly in the reign of Henry III, and they continued to live in this land uneasily until 1292 in the reign of Edward I.

The Jews were marked out for persecution because they were for the most part rich; and lest they should not be recognized immediately they were required to wear on their breasts, pieces of white linen or parchment attached to their outer garment.

This in itself was not enough, and the Archbishop of Canterbury, assisted by the Bishop of Lincoln, forbade any person to buy of Jews or sell to them any of those commodities which were necessary to the preservation of life. They were, declared these men of God, excommunicated by the Church, not only because they practised usury, but because they were not Christians.

Henry III was more lenient than his clergy and, when the Jews appealed to him, had sent forth a proclamation that all people who refused to sell goods to Jews, as the Church had commanded, should themselves be imprisoned.

It must have been very galling to the Church to see how these monarchs set themselves against it and insisted on ruling. However, the strip of water set the obstinate little island apart from other European countries, and the edict of the King was obeyed, with the result that the Jews lived peacefully in England for seven years.

Unfortunately for them, when unmolested they grew richer, and Henry began to think that he would like some of their wealth for himself; so a new law was made which proclaimed that one third of the wealth of every Jew must pass to the crown.

Nor was this all. Henry had given permission for the Jews to build a very splendid synagogue and, no sooner was the building completed, than he took possession of it, that it might be converted into a Christian Church.

Then in the year 1230 began a series of extortions which increased yearly to immense proportions; so that from 1265 to 1273 they paid over a sum of four hundred and twenty thousand pounds – worth a great many times the value of that sum today.

The Jews naturally protested at being thus penalized for their talents in making money, but the more complaints they made the more were taxes raised; and, when they began to find life in the country intolerable and thought of emigrating, they were, since they provided the exchequer with such a big source of income, forbidden to do so.

The people, seeing with what ease the King extracted money, looked about them for similar means of enriching themselves. It was a simple matter to fabricate tales about the Jews which would provide excuses for looting their houses and robbing them of their wealth. There were stories of Christian children being kidnapped and circumcised; worse still some of these children, it was alleged, had been crucified as an insult to the beliefs of Christians. Violence broke out and the Jews, bowed down by taxation, forbidden to leave the country and subjected to brutalities by the people, lived in great fear.

With the coming of the next King, Edward I, there was a big step towards modern times which was perhaps more discernible in England than in any other country. The English people began to show those characteristics which have been their strongest through the ages: a love of liberty and a determination to make their rulers feel the power of public opinion. But for this, Mary I, when she married Philip of Spain, might have established the Inquisition in these islands. Thanks to the spirit of the English, although her reign is darkened by the terrible fires of Smithfield, and those of other places in England, she was unable to do so.

With the coming of the strong Edward I to replace weak Henry III, it appeared that the Jews might expect better treatment. Edward, however, soon showed himself to be even harsher than his father. During his reign taxes continued to be levied, the Jews were confined to certain areas, and officers were appointed to assess the value of their possessions and tax them accordingly.

As if this were not enough, after he had been King for seven years, Edward brought in the death penalty for any Jew who was heard to question the divinity of Christ. This naturally struck at the root of their religion; and how easy it was for any who bore a grudge to bear witness against them!

Certain Dominican friars, no doubt in an endeavour to bring the Inquisition into the land, went among the Jews in the hope, they declared, of converting them to Christianity; and, under pain of punishment, they were forced to attend the sermons given by the monks.

A new law proclaimed that any Jew who became a Christian should immediately relinquish all his worldly goods to the crown; thus if a Jew sought to live in safety he must forfeit his goods. Jews apparently loved their possessions as much as the gentiles coveted them, and there were few converts; and no doubt because the wily King hoped for conversions and the accompanying benefits to his coffers, he relaxed the law a little and declared that converted Jews should not be compelled to abandon *all* their possessions.

Jews were continually being accused of crimes; and a favourite one was clipping coins, which was punishable by death. Many Jews suffered. Not only were they subjected to the excessive and unfair taxation by the state, but private people, we are told, made a great profit by extorting large sums as payment for *not* accusing them of some crimes.

Further measures were taken against them. One night, in all cities, officers of the law were sent into the Jewish quarters and many Jews were arrested and put into prison; they were only released on payment of a large ransom.

It may have been that so impoverished had the Jews become that they could no longer provide the great source of income which they had hitherto, for by the year 1290 the country was clamouring for their expulsion.

This Edward agreed to; he even allowed them to take a few of their possessions with them, although their houses and lands were seized by the crown; he also arranged that they should have protection from the mob.

They suffered greatly and must have been glad to leave a country which had treated them so badly; yet they would have known that they were unlikely to be received with any hospitality wherever they settled.

Holinshead tells a story of the exodus of the Jews which gives an idea of the attitude of the people towards them.

A party of very rich Jews on their departure hired a big ship to carry them away from England. They loaded it with the possessions which they could take with them and sailed down the Thames with it. The Captain of the ship cast anchor on pretext of waiting for a wind, and as the tide ebbed the ship grounded on the dry sand. As they must stay there some time, said the Captain, a little exercise would be good for them, and he invited the Jews to leave the ship and walk with him on the sand. He must have commiserated with them and made them believe he was their friend; but the crafty man had his eyes on the tide and, at a certain moment when he knew the ship could be refloated, was hauled up by a rope. The Jews, attempting to follow him, were too late to do so; and the Captain, from the safety of his ship, asked them why they did not call on their God, as Moses had done, to divide the water.

The Jews now unable to return to the land, where hostile people waited for them, made an effort to reach the ship which contained their treasure, but all were drowned in the attempt.

The Captain, Holinshead tells us, returned with the treasure to the King, and for this he was thanked and rewarded.

However, the historian does add that many others who behaved in such a manner were by no means rewarded and 'more truly as should seem' were hanged for their fraudulent conduct.

Thus the Jews were expelled from England and were not allowed to return until the days of Oliver Cromwell.

There are, to our shame, many cases of religious persecution in England but in later years nothing so terrible as that which occurred during the reign of Bloody Mary.

The times were violent; life was not held in the same respect as it is today; and we can be proud that public opinion played a big part in keeping the Inquisition – apart from that one instance of the persecution of the Knights Templar – from our shores.

In Norway and Sweden the Inquisition, happily, never appeared, but there was one country where it was received and flourished to such an extent that it was to become known throughout the world as The Spanish Inquisition.

CHAPTER FOUR

SPAIN BEFORE THE RECONQUEST

Why should Spain have been the country to embrace the Inquisition so wholeheartedly? Perhaps the answer is to be found by looking back to the very beginning of its recorded history.

Spain was a much-conquered country; from earliest times it had been the prey of invaders. It might have been that Ferdinand and Isabella, and those who came after, never lost sight of this, and that it was for this very reason that they nourished the Inquisition in their land that it might be a means of upholding not only the Catholic religion but the State.

The population, it appears, were originally Iberians and Tartesians; the Iberians living in the north, the Tartesians in the south. There was in these very early days some infiltration from the Celtic race which drifted in from France in the north, and from Great Britain in the west; thus before the appearance of the first conquerors there was probably a population of Iberians in the east, Celts in the north and west, with a Celtic influence on the Iberians in the centre of the country who were called Celtiberians.

Spain's geographical position made her vulnerable. She could be reached by land from the east; and Africa was within easy striking distance in the south. This no doubt accounts for the advent of so many colonizers and conquerors.

The Phoenicians were obviously a very adventurous people far in advance of their times, for not only were they enterprising traders, but peaceful ones. They were fortunate in being in possession of a country which was rich in natural resources. This land on the eastern shore of the Levant was a very small one, and no doubt it was for this reason that the Phoenicians decided on colonization.

They were Semitic in origin – traders, not fighters; they made glass, metal goods and dyes which must have seemed miraculous to the primitive peoples to whom they determined to sell their wares.

The Phoenicians were clearly of a civilization far in advance of their times, for not only did they sail the seas with a skill which was as remarkable as that which they displayed in the manufacture of their goods, but they produced an alphabet. This, it is said, was not an original one, but possibly adapted from the Egyptian; yet it is clear that these people had a great effect on the world.

They brought knowledge with their goods; and what is so remarkable is the picture of those primitive peoples gathering on the shore at the approach of a Phoenician vessel with something like the feeling that people in the last century, living in remote places, felt at the sight of the pedlar: pleasure and excitement devoid of fear.

Such an enterprising race could not be expected to remain in one small country; colonization was inevitable and, as those into whose lands they penetrated had learned that they had nothing to fear and much to gain from these peaceful traders, colonization continued on peaceful lines.

All along the Mediterranean coast they settled, bringing prosperity to their adopted lands, teaching the manufacture of glass and the making of their famous Tyrian purple dye, named after their city, Tyre, which was captured in 332 B.C. by Alexander the Great. In 850 B.C. they founded Carthage, which was their most important colony; it grew to such strength and power that it became more important than the homeland. Situated in North Africa on a peninsula not far from Tunis, Carthage was in a position to dominate Mediterranean shipping; and so important did it eventually become that it threatened Rome itself in the Punic wars until it was destroyed by Scipio in 146 B.C.

In Spain the Phoenicians settled in Malaga, Cadiz, Calpë (Gibraltar) and other towns in the south; and the Phoenicians were followed in this peaceful colonization by the Greeks.

Peace however did not continue, and the Tartesians of the south sought to drive the Phoenicians who had settled in Cadiz, from that town. The Phoenicians called in the help of those who had settled in Carthage, with the result that the Tartesians were driven back; but the Carthaginians, who had suffered heavy losses in the first of the Punic wars, decided that they would make up for these by the conquest of Spain.

The Spaniards, however, while they had been willing to receive the peaceful Phoenicians and Greeks, were determined not to surrender their land to the ambitious men of Carthage. The struggle to keep the invader out of Spain had begun.

Hamilcar Barca, the great Carthaginian general, who had fought in Sicily, led the invaders and defeated two chieftains, one Celtic, the other Celtiberian; Hamilcar's intention was to invade Italy by way of the Alps. However, not sooner had Hamilcar firmly planted his feet in Spain than another Iberian chief gathered together an army and, at Elche, Hamilcar's men were defeated and he himself killed in battle.

With Hamilcar in Spain was his son, the famous Hannibal, another son Hasdrubal, and his son-in-law also named Hasdrubal, all of whom were to play a part in Spain's history.

Hasdrubal, son of Hamilcar, won great victories in Spain in the year 212 B.C. and later commanded the Carthaginian army in Italy; he was killed at the battle of Metaurus in 207; the second Hasdrubal, Hamilcar's son-in-law who, on the death of Hamilcar, became the administrator of Spain and established Carthaginian power in the south of the peninsula, was murdered by one of his slaves in the year 221 B.C.

Hannibal, determined on the subjugation of the whole of Spain, laid siege to Saguntum, that city which destroyed itself rather than fall to the enemy; and the result of the battle for it led to the second Punic war and the famous march across the Pyrenees and the Alps into Italy. Hannibal's adventurous life terminated when he poisoned himself in 183 B.C. rather than fall into the hands of his enemies.

His failure in the second Punic war brought the Romans into Spain; and once again the natives of the troubled country were subject to an invader.

They were no more willing to accept the Romans than the Carthaginians, and in the first years they put up great resistance. But the highly civilized Romans soon proved themselves more than a match for the people of the Iberian peninsula, and, as they had no wish to spoil the country by fire and pillage, and antagonize the people by cruelty, a compromise was quickly reached. The people of Spain began to acquire the culture of their conquerors, as had other invaded peoples before them.

While Spain was under Roman control, Christianity was brought to the country, and this the Spaniards assimilated with Roman culture; as the years passed they produced poets, philosophers and statesmen to compare with the Romans.

There is the case of the poet Martial (Marcus Valerius Martialis) who was born in Bilbilis and went to Rome to become the favourite of both Nero and Domitian, who admired his poems and witty, if somewhat risqué, epigrams. There is also Lucan of Cordova who in Rome proved himself to be such a good poet that Nero was jealous of him and caused him to be banished; his life was a short one and he did not reach his thirtieth year for, joining in a conspiracy against Nero he was caught and, rather than fall into the hands of the tyrant, caused his veins to be opened and bled to death in his bath. Had he not been as good a poet as he was he might have lived longer; but his existence is proof of the acceptance of Roman culture by the people of Spain.

And if more evidence is needed, there is Lucius Annaeus Seneca himself, uncle of Lucan; brought from his native Cordova when he was a child, the philosopher was given the dangerous post of tutor to Nero, and although he accumulated great riches during the course of his duties he, like his nephew, was accused of conspiracy, ordered to kill himself and ended as Lucan did by opening his veins that he might bleed to death. There was also his father, Marcus Annaeus Seneca, who became a tutor of rhetoric in Rome.

Rome was even governed by an emperor who was of Spanish birth. This was Marcus Ulpius Trajan, given the succession by Nerva on account of his calm wisdom. Trajan was a persecutor of Christians, but he did not pursue this policy with the fanaticism of the Dominicans; he believed the Christians to be politically dangerous, and for that reason only did he persecute them.

It is obvious therefore that the Roman conquerors were acknowledged by the people of Spain to have brought them many advantages, and that there was no discrimination in Rome against Spaniards.

The Huns, that breed of barbarians who had invaded Europe in the fourth century, now came again in the fifth under their leader Attila. They were Mongolians, noted for their cruelty, and the Germanic peoples fled before them, invading Italy and Spain.

The Romans had become effete, and disaster overtook their once mighty Empire.

The Vandals swept on to Spain destroying the treasures of Rome and those of every town through which they passed. They established themselves in Baetica which was renamed Vandalusia – the Andalusia of today – but after a while they left Spain for Africa.

Then came the Visigoths – Western Goths – led by their King, Alaric, who had passed through Greece and Rome on his triumphant way.

The Visigoths settled in north-east Spain which was then called Gotha-landia, later to become Catalonia; those other invaders, the Suevians, were forced, on account of their fierce neighbours, to remain more or less shut up in Galicia.

Attila, called the Scourge of God because he inspired great terror wherever he appeared, was, after he had over-run the Roman Empire from which he had demanded enormous tribute, eventually defeated near Châlons-sur-Marne in a battle in which Goths, under Theodoric, joined with the Romans. Attila died in 453 on the day of his marriage; he was buried with great secrecy, so we are told, in a golden coffin in which had been placed fabulous treasures; and the slaves who had dug his grave were afterwards murdered lest they should disclose the secret.

But with Attila dead and Euric, the King of the Visigoths reigning over the land, the kingdom of Visigothic Spain had begun.

Religious differences arose within the kingdom, for the Hispano-Romans were Catholics and determined to cling to their faith.

Meanwhile the Franks had settled in Gaul, but thirty years after the famous battle of Châlons-sur-Marne, they still consisted of a nation of tribes, two of the principal of which were the Salian Franks and Ripuarian Franks.

Meroveus was the principal chieftain of the Salian Franks; and his son Childéric was father of Clovis I who became the founder of the Kingdom of France.

Clovis proved himself to be a stalwart warrior whom his followers could both fear and respect. When he decided that he wished to marry, his choice fell on Clotilde who was a niece of Gondebaud the King of Burgundy. She was reputed to be of great beauty and wisdom, but it might have been that the chivalry of Clovis was aroused by the peril in which she lived.

Her uncle the King, jealous of his brother Chilpéric, had had him and his two sons put to death. Agrippina, the wife of Chilpéric, had had a stone tied about her neck and been thrown into the Rhône; but Clotilde and her sister Chrona had escaped; Chrona had entered a nunnery, but Clotilde had fled to Geneva where she lived a very pious life.

There is a romantic story of how Clovis, unable to approach Clotilde on account of the jealous anger of her uncle Gondebaud, sent the Roman, Aurelian, in rags as a beggar, to her with a ring and a message that he, Clovis, wished to make her his wife.

Clotilde was delighted, and advised the Roman to return with all speed to Clovis and bid him demand her hand from her uncle.

This was done and Gondebaud, who dared not refuse such a powerful man as Clovis had become, sent for his niece and, after a marriage by proxy, she was allowed to leave with much treasure for Clovis's domain.

Clotilde, who was undoubtedly as wise as she was reputed to be, begged those who were taking her to her husband to make all speed as she feared her uncle might repent his benevolence. She was right in this because when Aridius, adviser of Gondebaud, returned from a journey which he had made to Marseilles and heard what had been done, he advised Gondebaud to set out after his niece and bring her back. Gondebaud retorted that he was delighted that a bond of friendship had been made by this marriage between him and the Franks; but he was then reminded of the murder of Clotilde's father, mother and brothers and warned that she would avenge them.

Gondebaud, seeing the wisdom in this, despatched troops to bring her back, but he was too late; and Clotilde, determined to avenge her family, had already instructed her escorts to burn and pillage Gondebaud's land as they passed through it.

The romantic story however is frowned on by the more sober historians. They suggest that Clovis asked Gondebaud for the hand of his niece Clotilde and Gondebaud agreed, not daring to offend the powerful Franks.

The marriage though was important historically because the Franks were pagans and Clotilde was Christian.

When their first son was born, Clotilde, who like most Christians, was burning with the desire to make all those about her accept her faith – and what was more natural than that she should desire her husband to do so more than any other? – wanted the boy to be baptized. There was evidently some controversy about this, for although Clovis was lenient concerning his wife's religion he was eager that his son should have the best gods working on his behalf.

Clotilde must have been very persuasive for she won, and the boy was baptized. Unfortunately for Clotilde the child died almost immediately. This brought forth reproaches from Clovis who was certain that if the boy had been dedicated to *his* gods he would have lived.

Another son was born, and again Clotilde prevailed on her husband to allow the child to have Christian baptism. Almost immediately the child fell sick. Clovis raged. This was *her* god, he cried. Such a god was clearly powerless.

Clotilde, however, prayed fervently and watched over the child, determined that he should live; and he did. Clovis was impressed for the little boy had been very ill indeed; but he still remained aloof from Christianity in spite of Clotilde's urgent pleas that he should accept it.

In 496 the Allemannians, a race of Germanic origin from the

73

Rhine, invaded the territory of the Franks. These Allemannians had the reputation of being fierce fighters and, according to the romantic chroniclers, before setting out to do battle, Clovis, who was certainly uneasy, told his wife that if he beat the Allemannians, he would accept her religion.

The point was that Clovis was eager not to be off with the old gods before he was on with the new, and he was very uncertain during the battle at Tolbiac near Cologne.

Aurelian, the Roman who had been his messenger and who was a Christian, was at his side; and when the battle was going against the Franks, he urged Clovis to become a Christian before it was too late.

Clovis is reputed to have cried: 'Jesus Christ, Thou who art the God of my wife Clotilde, I have prayed to my own gods and they have withdrawn from me. I invoke Thee. If Thou wilt give me the victory over my foes and if I find Thee to be as powerful as I have heard Thou art, then will I believe in Thee and be baptized in Thy name.'

The battle turned in Clovis's favour; the Allemannians were thoroughly beaten and their King slain.

As in Clovis's view the God of Clotilde had so clearly proved His mettle, he no longer put off his conversion; he was baptized by St Remi, Bishop of Rheims; and there was great rejoicing throughout the Catholic community.

The conversion of a powerful leader such as Clovis had its effect throughout his kingdom. His sisters, Alboflède and Lantéchilde, were baptized, and three thousand men in Clovis' army were also received into the Catholic Church. Pope Anastasius II was delighted and sent his congratulations.

Clovis, however, had lost none of his ambition; after all he had chosen what he believed to be the more powerful God on the battlefield. He thereupon turned to Burgundy and, defeating Gondebaud and setting up his rule there, he looked for fresh conquests; and his plans included the kingdom of Alaric II the Visigoth whose possessions, as well as those he held in Spain, included Aquitaine.

So Clovis set out to do battle with the Visigoths, but as he marched he did not forget his new religion, and he forbade his troops to pillage the country through which they passed; they might take only grass and water. There is a story that one of his soldiers, coming upon a poor man among his hay, stole his hay, declaring that hay was grass; but when Clovis heard of what happened, he drew his sword and cut off the head of the man who had taken the hay. 'What hope have we of victory,' he demanded, 'if we offend the saints?'

The battle took place at Poitiers where the Visigoths were at a disadvantage from the first, because they had only missiles with which to fight; and the Franks mowed through them with their swords. Clovis with his own hands slew Alaric; and the Visigoths retreated.

Clovis probably dreamed of taking his conquests south into Spain, but Theodoric of Italy had sent men to the aid of Alaric, who was his son-in-law; and Clovis was too wise to hazard all he had gained by taking his armies too far afield. So he made his way to Paris (taking Angoulême on his way) and set up his capital there.

He became the first King of France and established the Christian Faith in that land. He died in the year 511 and was buried in the church which had been built by his wife Clotilde (then called the Church of St Peter and St Paul, and later to be known as St Génevière).

The Christians in Spain were strengthened by the advent of a Christian neighbour, and during the troublous years to come the Kings of France were the allies of the Catholics in Spain; it may well have been that the knowledge of a powerful Christian neighbour kept the Christian Faith alive, in spite of the overwhelming presence of the Visigoths with their Arianism, and so prepared that flame which was, ten centuries later, to flare into the intolerance and bigotry which nourished the Inquisition.

Christianity in the Visgoth kingdom spread to the royal family and provoked a civil war. Leovigild, the King, had united the country and made it politically stronger than it had ever been; but his son Hermengild, afterwards St Hermengild, became a Christian and when, during the conflict between the Christians and the Arians he put himself at the head of the Christian army, he was defeated in battle; he suffered the martyr's death when he refused to accept the Arian belief.

When his brother Recared became King, he in his turn accepted Christianity at Toledo in 589. Recared was a strong man and the result of his conversion was that the Catholic clergy began to rise to a position of importance in the country. Recared grew rich; he loved comfort and learning; and it was during his reign that seats of culture were established in Toledo and Seville.

In the early part of the seventh century Isidore, Bishop of Seville, distinguished himself with his preaching and writings; and this man, in addition to his philosophical and theological work, wrote a history of the Visgothic kingdom.

The Christians were fast becoming a strong force within Spain; and eventually marriages between Latins and Goths were permitted. There were however many Jews in Spain, and their presence caused a great deal of friction, for wherever they appeared they seemed to be the victims of persecution.

They were accused of allying themselves with the enemies of the country and given a year to leave or become converts to Christianity. Many of them were baptized (some records say as many as 90,000) but it was inevitable that, with such an alternative before them, there were many pretended conversions to Christianity, while the rites of Judaism were practised in secret. And who can blame them for that?

The Visigothic kingdom, designed on Roman lines, appeared to follow the Roman pattern. After years of struggle within the kingdom and peaceful state of living had been attained; there was culture and prosperity, but it seemed, as in the Roman Empire before them, that this state of affairs produced a lethargy, a carelessness, an overfondness for a luxurious and easy way of life.

Meanwhile Carthage was 'blotted out' and every Christian stronghold in Africa was lost. Triumphant Islam was now very close to the Visigothic kingdom. The rulers of Spain seemed unaware that they might find it impossible to go on with their easy mode of living; they continued blindly in splendid palaces which included their harems. Everywhere was luxury and comfort calculated to appeal to the senses.

Sisebut, one of the Kings who had taken the extreme methods against the Jews, had expelled many of them, and these had settled among the Berbers of Africa; Sisebut's cruelty to this much persecuted race brought its reward, for the expelled Jews became the allies of the Berbers and naturally could give to a potential enemy information about the land they had vacated.

Soon after the fall of Carthage those Jews who remained in Spain, finding their position there intolerable and being fully aware of the lethargy into which the state had fallen, staged a rising which if successful, was to be the means of bringing back to Spain their exiled brethren.

It is thought that the expatriated Jews in Africa may have persuaded the Berber tribesmen to give them their aid.

This plot was discovered before the Jews had time to carry it out; the result was, naturally, increased harshness towards the Jewish population within the kingdom.

Discontent continued; but the rulers did not modify their manner of living; and all about them their enemies were alert.

There is a romantic story concerning the cause of the Arab invasion and the crumbling of the Visigothic kingdom.

There may be some truth in it, but it is certainly not the only cause of the invasion. The stage was set; and the forces of destruction had been creeping nearer for many years; yet it may have been that disruption within the kingdom supplied the match which started the blaze.

The story goes that a high official of the land, a certain Count Julian, had a very beautiful daughter named Florinda.

It was the custom in Visigothic Spain – and it was to continue in the centuries to come – to send the sons and daughters of noblemen to the Court there to learn the manners and habits of the nobility.

Roderic, the King, who was luxury-loving as all Visigothic kings had become, and who doubtless had his harem in the palace, no sooner became aware of the growing charms of Florinda than he longed to add her to his collection of women.

It seems that Florinda was a virtuous girl, who had no intention of submitting. She therefore held out against the importunate King, which of course only increased his ardour.

77

One day when Florinda went down to bathe in the Tagus, Roderic found her there, and raped her.

This may have seemed a trivial incident in the life of a sybarite king, but Florinda had no intention of accepting such treatment without protest and she hurried to her father, Count Julian, to tell him what had taken place.

Julian, incensed at the deflowering of his daughter, swore he would revenge himself upon the King; so he went to Tangiers where Tarik governed for the Moslems in the name of the great ruler Mousa. Julian told Tarik that although the plans for the attack on Spain had previously failed, if Tarik tried again he might be successful. King Roderic was weakened by luxurious and riotous living, and he, Julian, would place himself on the side of Tarik and give him all the information at his disposal. He would help him bring about the downfall of Roderic's kingdom because, since Roderic had violated his daughter, he was determined on his destruction.

Tarik, delighted to have secured the cooperation of Julian, immediately began making plans, and with the help of the angry Count many Arab soldiers were smuggled into Spain to await and assist the landing of the invading forces when they should arrive.

Many historians, however, refuse to accept the story. It is too melodramatic. It is possible, they ask, that the rape of a girl could be responsible for the domination of Christian Spain by the Mussulman for more than seven centuries?

But the legend was preserved and at Toledo on the Tagus there are ruins which are known as the Baths of Florinda and it is at this spot that the rape is said to have taken place. There seems to be little doubt, moreover, that there was a Count Julian and that he betrayed his country.

Mousa must have been a cautious man for, in spite of the help offered by Count Julian, he decided first to send a small force to Spain to spy out the land; and this he did under the command of one of his freedmen, Tarif.

This happened in the year 710. Tarif landed opposite Tangiers, and the spot where he first set foot in Spain was thenceforth known as Tarifa. Tarif came with a very small force but he managed to penetrate as far as Algeciras; the expedition was meant to be only a raid, and Tarif contented himself with looting the houses of the inhabitants. He was able to show Mousa the sort of treasures and women which would be won if they carried an offensive war into Spain.

The treasures – and chiefly the women – so delighted Mousa that he determined to make further investigations, and this time they should be on a more ambitious scale.

Tarik was commanded to set out for Spain, not to make a raid as Tarif had done, but to establish a foothold that the Arabs might pour into the country.

He established his troops on a rock which was called the Gebel-Tarik (The mountain of Tarik) and which was to become known in the centuries to come as Gibraltar.

Hearing that the enemy had a foothold in his country, Roderic prepared to do battle; but he and his men had wasted a great deal of time in luxurious living and it was not easy to prepare themselves for the fierce Arabs in the time left to them. The army might be superior in numbers, but it lacked the fighting fervour of the Arabs. Moreover, now that a bridgehead had been established, it was possible for Tarik to add to his forces; he had Count Julian to advise him; and when the battle took place, it was so fierce that there were thousands of casualties in the Visigoth King's supporters, and Roderic himself must have been among them, for he disappeared and the manner of his dying was never discovered.

The battle won, the King dead, the Arabs lost no time in marching forward. They had not only the help of the enraged Julian, but also the active support of the Jews, who made it easy for them to take possession of the main cities of the south.

Mousa came to Spain to consolidate Tarik's triumphs; and gradually the south of Spain fell under the domination of the Mussulman.

Some of the Christians remained in their cities and accepted the Arab rule. They became known as Mozarabs – which meant that they, although retaining their Christian religion, were subjects of the Moorish Kings; but many left their homes for the mountains of the north. Here they remained aloof from the conquerors – in such areas as Navarre, Aragon, Catalonia and the Asturias; here they lived through the centuries, waiting for the day when they would drive the Infidel from their country.

Having completed the conquest of southern Spain, Mousa and his lieutenant Tarik would have preferred to return to Africa, for the Arabs were never lovers of the sea and were always apprehensive when it divided them from their homeland. However, Caliph Walid refused to allow them to do this. The Arab Empire was growing and it was the intention of the Arabs to enlarge it still further. What point was there in capturing land, plundering and then abandoning it? Southern Spain had become part of the Arab Empire and Mousa and his men must remain there. He and his soldiers were therefore given lands and property in the country and were told it was their duty to stay there, to govern the people, and keep this new acquisition within the Empire.

In the beginning there was tolerance towards the Christians, but there was naturally the usual strife and suspicions.

The Mozarabs were contemptuous of those who had become converted to Islam; and the Mussulmans were suspicious of them both.

Heavy taxes were imposed on Christians, who might find these relieved if they gave up their religion for that of the conquerors. It was the beginning of persecution, and a violent people such as the Arabs, to whom life was cheap, wasted little time in arguing.

Tarik was a conqueror; it was he and his forces who had made possible the successful occupation; he was however involved in a suspicion of having kept to himself certain monies and properties which by right belonged to his masters; and when Mousa and he met, instead of being received with the honours which a successful general might have expected, Mousa flourished a whip with which he began to beat Tarik; and when the astonished general was bleeding from the lashes, Mousa roared to his men to take Tarik away and shave his head so that all might know of his shame.

It was then that the conquered people must have realized the violence and cruelty of their conquerors. But the Arabs were not consciously cruel. They were barbaric and brutal by upbringing. Cutting off the heads from the bodies of enemies had seemed a reasonable act; and crucifixion was the recognized punishment meted out to those who had offended against their laws.

Arab chroniclers tell us that so eager were they for peace in the land they had conquered that Abd el Aziz, the son of Mousa, married the daughter (some say widow) of the defeated Roderic. She was a Christian and, if this actually happened, it must have had a very soothing effect on the conquered people.

It was not long before there was trouble, for the conquerors were made up of numerous tribes among whom there were perpetual rivalries. The Berbers, who had first come to Spain under Tarik, considered they had not had their fair shares of the spoils and, since they had done the hardest part of the work of conquest, they quickly grew dissatisfied. The haughty Arabs were contemptuous of them and determined to flaunt their own superiority. This gave rise to internal quarrels and, as they were by no means a gentle people, violent atrocities were committed on both sides. For instance, when a quarrel broke out between the ninety-year-old Abd el Malik and the Syrian Baldj, Abd el Malik was seized by Baldj's soldiers, beaten, cut with swords and crucified. As was the custom with crucifixion, animals were treated in the same manner at the same time, and on either side of the old man a pig and a dog were also crucified.

Meanwhile the Christians in the north were waiting, and between them and the Mussulman territory of the south was a no-man's-land, a desert to divide them. Each side was alert, unsure of the other; the Christians determined that some day they would regain their lost territory, the Arabs determined to hold what they had won.

It may have been that the continual quarrels would have brought disaster to Arab Spain but for the first of their great rulers, Abd er Rhaman.

The Arabs were a people who believed in destiny, and prophecy played a great part in their lives. In fact it may have been Abd er Rhaman's conviction that he was destined to be the saviour of Spain, that made him so; for when he was a very young child it was prophesied that he was destined to conquer

Spain, and this was believed by his family, and he himself was soon made aware of it.

His grandfather was the Caliph Hisham whose family were defeated and replaced by the Abbasides. Young Abd er Rhaman, who was in the palace when it was being looted, escaped with his young brother and hid in a nearby village; but the boys were betrayed, and soldiers came in pursuit of them with orders to kill them if they should be found.

Abd er Rhaman ran with his brother to the river's edge, the soldiers of their family's enemies close behind them. If they were to escape they must swim across the river, and they plunged in. Abd er Rhaman swam strongly, shouting encouragement to his brother who, unable to swim fast enough was caught by the soldiers who waded in after him.

From the other side of the river, where he stood in safety, young Abd er Rhaman saw the soldiers cut off the head of his brother.

This must have been a distressing sight, but Abd er Rhaman was an Arab; he believed in destiny; and as 'it was written' that he should rule Spain, so, he would have told himself, was it that his brother would fall into the hands of their enemies and perish, as had so many of his relations. After that the boy lived a wandering life, learning a great deal, suffering much hardship, never forgetting his destiny. In Kairouan he encountered the suspicions of Ibn Habib who had himself great ambitions and, doubtless hearing of the great destiny in store for Abd er Rhaman, was determined to remove him. Abd er Rhaman escaped with his life and arrived in Ceuta where he lived for a while among the Berbers (his mother was a Berber slave girl).

Across the straits were Gibraltar and Spain; it is certain that he had not forgotten his brilliant destiny, and it was not long before Abd er Rhaman was sending his spies into the country across the water to discover how he would be received if he should appear among them.

He discovered that the people were ready for him. Somail, leader of the Kaishites who had conquered the Yemenites and beheaded their chiefs in the Cathedral Square of Saint Vincent, was universally hated for his cruelty; and the Yemenites were ready to receive Abd er Rhaman as their new leader.

Abd er Rhaman knew however that it would not be a matter of defeating Somail only; there was the latter's powerful ally, Yousouf, and before attempting to land in Spain he tried to separate these two; failing to do this, yet so sure of himself, he arrived, ready to do battle, and he defeated the combined forces of Somail and Yousouf on the banks of the Guadalquivir.

Abd er Rhaman, as the outcome of that battle, became Emir of Spain. This took place in the year 756.

Determined to fulfil his destiny he set out to be completely independent of Bagdad; but it was not long before Yousouf rose against him. Yousouf was beaten, however, and *pour encourager les autres* Abd er Rhaman placed his head and that of his son on the bridge at Cordova.

Somail, who had also revolted, was captured and imprisoned. But Abd er Rhaman had no intention of letting this enemy live, so he was strangled in his prison.

This however was not the end of Abd er Rhaman's troubles. The Yemenites, who had supported him because they hated Somail and Yousouf, now considered that they had been denied their full share of the spoils of conquest; therefore when urged to revolt by the Caliph El Mansour, one of the Abbasides who had taken the Caliphate from Abd er Rhaman's family, they were willing to do so. As a result Abd er Rhaman was besieged in Carmona. However his certainty in his destiny seemed to inspire him with great vigour, for he defeated the rebels, had their leaders beheaded and sent their heads salted and stuffed with myrrh to El Mansour.

Other rebels were stripped of their clothes which were replaced by rags, their heads were shaved, and they were made to ride on donkeys through the city of Cordova to a hill whereon crosses had been set up. There, to provide a spectacle for the citizens which was meant to be both an entertainment and a lesson, they were crucified.

Abd er Rhaman fulfilled his destiny; he had established the Caliphate in Spain; he was triumphant over all his enemies, although it was necessary for him to fight against them all his life. Tall, fair something of a poet, he who had been driven from his own kingdom had succeeded in planting his dynasty in a new one. He was the father of only twenty children – not many according to Arab standards – and this was probably due to the fact that he spent a great deal of time in war instead of with his harem. He must have been a somewhat cultured man, and it is unfortunate that he was forced to spend so much of his time in fighting. It was during his reign that culture began to flower; and in 786 he began to build the mosque in Cordova which was to become the cathedral and is one of the most magnificent examples of Arab architecture.

The Emirs and Caliphs at first respected the religion of the Mozarab Christians, but with the reigns of Abd er Rhaman II and his son Mohammed I persecution set in.

There were many Catholics in Cordova, and in the neighbourhood there was no lack of churches and monasteries; it may have been that the sight of the Christians' growing numbers alarmed the Arabs, for they began to look about them for Christian martyrs.

The Christians appeared to make no attempt to avoid martyrdom; in fact they seemed to seek it, and Abd er Rhaman II was so annoyed by this that he declared that those Christians who sought martyrdom should be denied it; and as a result the persecution ceased temporarily. However, Abd er Rhaman's son, Mohammed I, determined to renew it; and he did.

Meanwhile, with a long sojourn in an alien land, the character of the Arabs was undergoing a change. They had been hard fighters, nomads, unaccustomed to luxury; but the climate of Southern Spain sapped their vitality; they began to crave for luxury, and lived in idleness, surrounded by their harems.

They lived dangerously. There were the Hispano-Visigoths, who had been driven into the north, for ever ready to descend upon them and win back what they had lost; but perhaps most dangerous were the warring elements in their own midst.

There were many risings against the Caliphate, and one of the most terrible and the most typical was that which occurred on the accession of Hakam I.

Hakam's father was the serious-minded Hisham I who had followed Abd er Rhaman I in 788; and during the reign of Hisham I a Berber *faquis*, Yahya ben Yahya, had risen to prominence, and on the death of Emir Hisham, this man stated that Hakam was unfit to rule. He was not, declared Yahya ben Yahya, serious enough to follow the pious Hisham, being too fond of the pleasures of bed and board.

Hakam quickly discovered the plot, arrested about seventy of those concerned, and had them publicly crucified. Yahya ben Yahya escaped to Toledo where he was given refuge.

The people of Toledo had always sought to hold themselves aloof from the Arabs, and there were many Christians living in the city.

Hakam, not wishing to make war on Toledo, was yet determined to show the city that he intended to be its master. He appointed a new governor to the town, who was not an Arab; this delighted the people of Toledo, for they did not know that Hakam had arranged with the new governor that all the most important people of the town should be murdered.

The new governor, on secret instructions from Hakam, had an alcázar built in the town; it was proposed to use it for troops who would protect the city.

When it was built, a great feast was given in it to all the notable people of Toledo. To reach the alcázar it was necessary to cross the courtyard in which a ditch had been dug while the building was being erected; there was chalk and clay in this ditch.

Seven hundred of the town's most important citizens were invited, so say some Arab sources (others declared it was not more than 500) and as they were admitted, one by one they were escorted across the courtyard to the building. Soldiers were standing at attention beside the ditch and as each guest passed, a soldier would raise his sword and cut off the guest's head. Bodies and head were then thrown in to the ditch.

It was an Arab custom to pile up in heaps the heads and sometimes the bodies of their victims; this was their method of assessing the size of a victory.

The affair of the ditch subdued the Toledans and the agitator, Yahya ben Yahya, but the latter continued to preach against Hakam, and the citizens of Toledo did not forget the affair of the ditch.

Six years later there was another rising, this time in the suburb of Secunda on the bank of the Guadaquivir, and Hakam was determined to sow fear in the hearts of all rebels this time. So he made up his mind that he would burn the suburb of Secunda.

First, however, three hundred of the suburb's most important people, who were suspected of being leaders of the revolt, were arrested and crucified heads downwards; the crosses had been set up along the river bank opposite the Bridge of Cordova.

The people of Secunda were forced to witness the slow death agonies of the three hundred before they were driven from their homes and banished from Spain. Hakam then set fire to every house.

Surely that must have been one of the most terrible scenes in history: three hundred men dying in lingering agony, watched by those who were being driven with whips from their burning homes.

The change in the character of the Arabs of Spain began to show itself in the tenth century. Their palaces were becoming more luxurious and Abd er Rhaman II went so far as to have water brought to his palace.

Abd er Rhaman III, who came nearly a hundred years later, was also a great builder, and spent much time, when he was not fighting, in producing mosques and palaces, or embellishing those he already had. His most spectacular achievement was the palace of Medina az Zahara which was built for his favourite, Zahara, and named after her.

Meanwhile the Christians in the country were living very precarious and dangerous lives.

Those who had remained in Arab territory were obliged to live together in certain quarters, as the Jews did in their ghetto; it may have been that they preferred this to living free of Arab domination in the north, for life there was one of poverty and uncertainty. There was continual war because, fearful of attacks from the north, the Arabs perpetually attacked; and twice yearly an army was sent north to harry the Christians, to destroy their churches, to burn their crops and to steal their women and children that they might be sold as slaves.

The Christians were on the defensive for centuries, but Alfonso III, King of the Asturias, who came to the throne in 866 secured many victories over the enemy. This was a sign. The Christians, living their hard lives in the north, were growing stronger; the Arabs were growing weaker through excesses in their grand palaces. Alfonso died in 910, but although he had shown that it was possible to win victories over the Moors, this merely produced a stirring of resentment against the oppressor; and with the coming of strong rulers such as El Mansour, the usurper of the Caliphate, the Christians lost any advantage they had gained. This man, who had one of his own sons whipped to death in his presence for some misdemeanour, was unlikely to show leniency towards his enemies.

It was El Mansour who, after a battle which brought him thirty thousand Christian prisoners, ordered them all to be decapitated, their heads and bodies piled high; and from the top of this great human mound the muezzin chanted his call to prayer. On another occasion after a victory he returned to Cordova with thousands of Christian prisoners carrying the spoils of the battle through the streets, and those spoils were the treasures of their own churches.

But in the year 1043 there was born the man who was to show that what could be done by the conquerors could be done by the conquered; and it was this man who has a place of honour in Spanish history, because he roused the conquered people from their lethargy. I refer to Roderigo de Vivar who is better known as the Cid Campeador.

He was born in Vivar, that little village not far from Burgos, which in the days of the Cid's childhood was on the border and in danger of being ravaged each spring and autumn by the Caliph's punitive forces.

The Cid was left an orphan when he was in his early teens and, because his mother was a member of a noble Asturian family, he was sent to the court of the Infante Don Sancho to be given the upbringing which was accorded to children of the nobility.

He proved himself to be more interested in the art of war than in culture, but he was by no means illiterate; the young boy, who would doubtless have witnessed the cruelty meted out to his people by the Arabs, may have been fired then by a determination to dedicate his life to the deliverance of those people.

There have, of course, been many romantic stories concerning this man; and it is difficult to discover what he was really like. Those who would depreciate him tell us that he was a rough soldier, unlettered, almost barbaric; in the Spanish poems and plays which have been written about him he emerges as a romantic lover, handsome and cultured, almost a saint.

It may be true that, when he took prisoners at the siege of Valencia, some of those prisoners were torn to pieces by hungry dogs and others burned alive. Even so, it is necessary to consider the amount of barbaric cruelty the Cid must have witnessed. It must also be borne in mind that whatever else he was, he was a man of his times, that he was fighting a great battle against the oppressor, and that he, even as Ferdinand and Isabella, is responsible for the reconquest of Spain.

He fought with the Infante Sancho at Graus and later was made *Alférez* of Castile when Sancho was King; this meant that he was in command of Sancho's army, so it is clear that his military genius was apparent at an early age.

A melodramatic legend about his marriage to Jimena tells how he killed her father in a duel because he opposed the match; this may well be false and the marriage purely one of convenience.

Sancho had been killed by his brother Alfonso at the time the marriage took place; and, probably because Sancho's friends would not find much favour with the brother who had supplanted him, the Cid lost his post of *Alférez*. But Alfonso would have realized the merits of this man and, not wishing to offend him, arranged the marriage which, from the Cid's point of view, was a good one. For he, although his mother was of a noble house of the Asturias, was the son of a humble father, and Jimena Díaz was the daughter of Count Oviedo and Alfonso's niece.

For ten years the Cid remained in obscurity; then began his life as a warrior.

His genius was apparent from the first and resulted in victory for the side on which he fought; his name became a legend; but Alfonso had always been suspicious of him, particularly as the Cid knew that it was Alfonso who had been responsible for the murder of Sancho; and he seized an opportunity of sending the Cid into exile, although he did not confiscate his goods.

So the Cid was forced to leave Jimena and his children at Vivar while he moved on with his followers. He was a soldier by profession and, presenting himself to the ruler of Barcelona, he offered to fight for him; when the offer was refused he made another to Moctadir who, though a Moor and King of Saragossa, was an ally of Alfonso; for there were occasions when Moors and Christians were allies against a common enemy.

Moctadir was quick to discover the worth of Cid; and so the Cid stayed at his court for several years, an honoured companion and adviser.

So famous did the Cid become, hailed everywhere as El Campeador, that he desired a kingdom of his own and eventually won Valencia for himself.

Valencia, it is said, was the great love of his life. He loved it, it is said, 'as lovers love the place where they have tasted the delights of love'. Jimena and his children joined him there and for four years, until he died, he was lord of the place.

When he died at the age of fifty-six, Jimena could not long hold Valencia and it was recaptured by the Mussulmans. It might have seemed then that all the victories which the Cid had won were of no account, since it was left to Ferdinand and Isabella four hundred years later to expel the Moors from Spain.

But the example of the Cid was to shine through the ages of oppression to come. He had proved that there *were* Spaniards from the north who could fight in such a manner as to subdue the conquerors. Even though the results of his conquests had been lost, his example remained.

The reconquest was certainly delayed by two further invasions, those of the Almoravides and the Almohades; and these invasions were entirely due to the people of Spain themselves. Afraid of the growing triumphs of Alfonso VI, which had been so advanced by the triumphs of the Cid, Christians and

Moslems alike, determined not to fall under the sway of the 'Emperor of the Christians', called in the help of the Almoravides, a Moslem dynasty which ruled from 1055 to 1147.

They must soon have realized the folly of this, for as the Almoravides swept over the country they behaved as conquerors. Motamid, the ruler of Seville, was taken prisoner and others were slain. The whole of the south was under one rule and the Christians in the north were more unhappy than they had previously been.

The Almoravides reigned until a new dynasty appeared in Africa; the Almohades, who in their turn invaded Spain and took possession of the southern land from 1129 to 1273.

It may have been that these two invasions, following on the vigorous example set by the Cid, made the Spaniards of the north realize that, unless they expelled the invader from their country for ever, they would be constantly subject to similar invasions; and that they themselves might one day be driven from their northern settlements. Surely it occurred to them then that there was only one course open to them. They must, if they were to enjoy any security, turn the invader from their country.

The Almohades were devotees of their faith, and they were greatly influenced by their *faquis*; they went into battle with the belief that it was the will of Allah that they should do so.

The Christians too had their belief. They had been long oppressed; but they had the glowing example of the Cid to guide them.

In July of 1212 they met the enemy at Las Navas de Tolosa; and the battle resulted in a victory for the Christians.

This was a significant date in the history of Spain, for it was a beginning.

Progress was slow, and it was not until 1236 that Ferdinand III captured Cordova; later Malaga and Seville fell into his hands; and his son, Alfonso X, continued with the conquests.

Saragossa was recovered, Valencia won back; and of the utmost strategic importance – Algeciras.

By the end of the fourteenth century the only part of Spain occupied by the Moors was the kingdom of Granada; and it seems incredible that Granada should have been allowed to remain in Moorish hands.

Granada, it was true, was well protected by the sierras; many of those who were antagonistic to the Christians had fled to Granada and settled there; hatred of the Christians had been brought to a higher pitch than ever; moreover, the rulers of this last stronghold were ready to call in help from Africa if they were attacked in any force.

Strife among the Christian kingdoms no doubt delayed the reconquest. Castile and Aragon were rivals for power; and while civil wars persisted the Moors remained secure in Granada.

It was not until Isabella of Castile and Ferdinand of Aragon united that the Moors were conquered. To these two sovereigns goes the credit of freeing Spain from the invader and uniting the country. To them also is attached the stigma of introducing the Inquisition into Spain.

It is, I feel, only by looking back over the early history of Spain that it is possible to understand why the Inquisition prospered there as in no other country. The Catholic sovereigns were determined to have a united country, and they did not believe this ambition could be achieved unless all their subjects accepted one religion. This they were determined to bring about through persuasion, if possible, and if not, by force.

Spain under Isabella and Ferdinand was ripe for the Inquisition; that was why the cruel institution was embraced so heartily and continued to survive until the nineteenth century.

CHAPTER FIVE

ISABELLA AND FERDINAND

When the early days of Isabella the Catholic are considered one understands why such a woman, of virtue and stern devotion to duty, was eventually persuaded to set up the Inquisition and use it as a means of strengthening the state.

Isabella was born on the 22nd April in the year 1451 in the town of Madrigal de las Altas Torres, into a world of uncertainty and conflict.

Her father's reign had been far from peaceful and she was not quite four years old when he died. John II had proved himself to be a weak King, and during his reign lawlessness had spread throughout Castile. The nobility were arrogant in the extreme and, since robbery and rape went unpunished, the goods and families of humble citizens were unsafe; and in many of the towns the honest men and women gathered together to try to discover a means of bringing law and order to the land.

John was completely in the hands of one of his favourites, Alvaro de Luna who, though illegitimate, belonged to one of the noble houses of Aragon. He was handsome, charming, fond of music, and a writer of poetry – all of which greatly appealed to the King, who made him Grand Master of St James and Constable of Castile.

Alvaro de Luna, insatiably ambitious, began to accumulate great treasure as he usurped the power from under the King's very nose. The nobles of Castile, who prided themselves on their aristocratic connections, were infuriated to witness the arrogance of this man and as a result there was continual strife throughout the kingdom, in which John's son, Henry, did not hesitate to join against his own father.

De Luna, believing himself to be above reproof, not only imposed heavy taxes but withdrew from the people all the privileges which had been won during the preceding years. Such a state of affairs could not go on indefinitely, and de Luna eventually met his death on the scaffold.

But in the meantime a great deal of harm had been done and, although King John supported the arts and had made his court a place of culture, because he was weak in matters of government and because he had placed himself in the hands of the scheming, if attractive, de Luna, his kingdom was in a state of anarchy at the time of his death.

His first wife was Maria of Aragon, and by her he had one son, Henry, who was heir to the throne. His second wife was the Princess Isabella, who was a granddaughter of John I of

Portugal, and by her he had two children; one of these was Alfonso; the other Isabella.

On his death-bed King John begged his son Henry to take great care of his young sister and brother, and this Henry swore he would do.

These two young children were taken from the Court to the little town of Arevalo in the care of their mother who guarded them and personally superintended their religious instruction. It was a very pious upbringing which fell to the lot of Isabella.

Their elder brother Henry was far from pious.

He was acclaimed with delight by his people who had long wearied of the futility of his father. The fact that Henry had placed himself among those who had stood in opposition to John gave the people great hope. Here was a young King, a man with new ideas, one who was known to have disapproved of the follies of his father.

Only a short period elapsed before the long-suffering people of Castile began to see that John had been slightly more admirable than his son.

Henry was determined to win popularity; he was of an equable temper and declared his determination to lead campaign after campaign against the Moors until they were driven out of Granada. He loved luxury; but he differed from his father inasmuch as he had no love for music or poetry.

He began his reign by delving deep into the royal coffers, and to all protests replied that Kings must be liberal; generosity ensured popularity for it was necessary to turn enemies into friends by the means of gifts, and to offer gifts to friends to keep them friendly. He enjoyed splendour and so increased his household. As for the promised forays against the Moors, he spent a great deal of money on these, but he liked the pomp and show of soldiering more than fighting; and, although he and his armies set out with shouting and fanfares of trumpets, they showed little desire for real fighting and would return after the briefest encounter with the enemy, which had cost his subjects much in taxes and had brought but derisive contempt from the Moors.

It was useless for him to say that he did not care to risk the lives of his men, since one Christian was worth a thousand Mussulmans. He had gathered together an army to fight, and that army consisted of nothing but men in fancy dress performing a masque for the King's entertainment.

It was at this time that the people began to ask themselves whether they had not been better ruled by King John II than by his son King Henry IV.

Henry who had indulged in sensual orgies from an early age, repudiated his wife, Blanche of Aragon, after they had been married for twelve years. There were no children of the marriage, and the excuse for rendering the marriage void was '*Por impotencia respectiva*, owing to some malign influence.' So was this woman turned from her husband's household to tragic fate, for Henry, if he was foolish, if he was a voluptuary, was at least of a benign temper, and the years she spent in Castile must have been some of the most bearable of her life.

Having rid himself of Blanche, Henry took a new wife. She was Joanna of Portugal who was sister of Alfonso V.

Joanna lacked the graceful manners which were considered so important in Castile; she was lighthearted and coquettish; and it was not long before she brought scandal into the court.

One of the handsomest men about her husband's throne was Beltran de la Cueva, and it soon became apparent that the new Queen found his company enthralling.

Henry, not to be outdone by his wife in providing scandal, had already shown a preference for one of the maids of honour whom she had brought in her train. This girl quickly made her influence felt at court, and the Queen, although she did not object to the girl's sharing her husband's attention, was determined to maintain her own power.

Thus very shortly after the arrival of the new Queen there was gossip, scandal and friction.

Money was needed to pay for the luxurious court, and more taxes were extorted; great sums were raised ostensibly for the campaigns against Granada, but were in reality used to satisfy the whims of the favourites of both King and Queen.

And while this was going on young Isabella was leading a quiet existence, with her brother Alfonso, praying at her mother's knee, being prepared for future greatness – which it must have occurred to Isabella's mother and those loyal supporters in her household – was not impossible, for who should take the throne on the King's death, if he died childless, but his brother Alfonso; or should he fail to reach maturity: Isabella.

Then the astonishing thing happened. Queen Joanna was pregnant.

From the beginning nobody believed that the father was Henry, and when the girl was born, because all were certain that she was the fruit of the passion between her mother and the favourite, Beltran de la Cueva, she was known (although named Joanna) as La Beltraneja. Henry, all believed, was impotent; and therefore could not be the father of the girl.

This gave rise to great scandal, for the unfortunate child, since she was the only one Henry possessed, was heir to the throne of Castile. Henry, in his easy-going manner taking the simplest way out of the difficulty, insisted that an oath of fealty be sworn to her and she be accepted as heir to the throne.

It was at this point that the young Alfonso, until now living quietly in the care of his mother, found interest focused upon him. Revolution was in the air; and although warned by his advisers to take sharp action, Henry procrastinated; he had no wish to shed blood over this matter. It might have been that he wanted to hush up the scandal which surrounded his court, and felt that the best way of doing this was to accept the little Beltraneja as his own.

Henry now summoned his sister Isabella and their brother Alfonso to court, on the pretext of supervising their education; but he must have done this because he realized that with the nobles in a state of ferment it was dangerous to allow the children to be anywhere but in his own court.

The scandal of Henry's private life was fast earning him contempt; but there was one other factor which was making him very unpopular, and that was his easy-going nature which allowed him to be led by those of his favourites on whom he doted.

Henry, realizing that his throne was in danger and that he

must make some concession to the nobles, named Alfonso as his heir on condition that he married La Beltraneja.

One important nobleman who was responsible for making a great deal of trouble was Juan Pacheco, Marquis of Villena. The Marquis had originally been a page in the household of the favourite, Alvaro de Luna, and when Henry was young Villena had been put into his service. Wily and ambitious Villena had quickly begun to dominate his master; and he was therefore furious when he saw new favourites ousting him from the King's regard.

So Villena determined to depose Henry and put Alfonso in his place.

Thus in the year 1465 the boy Alfonso was taken to a field near Avila where a platform had been set up; and on this was placed a chair in which was set an effigy of Henry in all his regalia. Alfonso Carillo, the Archbishop of Toledo, an uncle and ardent supporter of Villena, then mounted the platform and removed the crown from the effigy; Villena and his adherents took away the remains of the kingly splendour, and the effigy was thrown from the platform to the spectators, who with great pleasure rolled it in the dust.

Then eleven-year-old Alfonso was required to mount the platform and induced to be seated; the crown was placed on his head; homage was paid to him, and the people shouted that he was the new King.

Although this dramatic display was received with vociferous delight by the spectators, it was not regarded with approval by the rest of the country. Much as the conduct of Henry was deplored, he was still the King and could at that time have rallied his army about him and defeated the opposing party; but he was a lover of peace, and he sought to make conciliatory terms.

In the meantime there appeared to be two Kings of Castile – Henry and little Alfonso.

Characteristically Henry, realizing that the powerful Villena was his enemy, sought to make him his friend; and as Henry's idea of making friendship was to offer gifts, he now decided to win Villena to his side by a gift of such importance that he could not fail to proffer friendship in return for it.

Villena had a brother, Don Pedro Giron, Grand Master of the order of Calatrava; and to this brother was offered the hand of Isabella, who was at this time sixteen years old.

Henry believed that by such a marriage Villena must become his ally, and as his other enemy, the Archbishop of Toledo, was the uncle of the proposed bridegroom, he too would welcome the honours such a marriage would bring and replace with friendship the enmity he bore Henry.

Isabella had already been promised in marriage to three suitors – Ferdinand of Aragon, his elder brother Carlos and Alfonso of Portugal, and when the proposition was made to Isabella that she would marry the Grand Master she haughtily declined.

The marriage seemed to her most unsuitable; she had already made up her mind that alliance with Aragon would unite the kingdoms, and she was determined not to marry merely for a whim of her rather feeble-minded brother, Henry.

Imbued with the dignity and piety with which she had been surrounded in the quiet retreat of Arevalo, she replied that the nobles of Castile must be consulted before their infanta could be given in marriage.

However, she realized that she was powerless in the hands of the King. She was fully aware that the Grand Master, many years her senior, had during his lifetime indulged in the licentious behaviour which was characteristic of the court; and she is reputed to have retired to her apartments in deepest gloom, to have spent hours on her knees imploring the saints to save her from the marriage, going without sleep and food in her fear and grief, and declaring to her attendant, Beatriz de Bobadilla, that she would plunge a dagger into the heart of the Grand Master if he approached her.

All her entreaties were ignored and the bridegroom and his relations, delighted at the prospect of being connected with the royal family, set about preparations of such magnificence as had rarely been seen at the court before.

The bridegroom left his home in Almagro for Madrid where the wedding was to take place, and the first night of the journey was spent at Villarubia, where the bridegroom was suddenly attacked with a violent illness which it was difficult to diagnose. He became so ill that within four days he was dead.

It is not certain what or who brought about this timely death, but it seems very likely that the merry bridegroom had taken a dose of poison. He must have had many enemies, and Isabella many friends. There has never been any suggestion that the pious Isabella played a part in the removal of the man whom she had threatened to kill should he approach her.

Isabella was then free to make that other most important and most famous marriage and to earn for herself the distinction of bringing the Inquisition into Spain.

With the death of the Grand Master all the hopes of Villena and the Archbishop of glorification through marriage with the royal house were lost, and since there was nothing to be gained, they once more showed their enmity towards the King. Civil war broke out, and at the head of the rebels side by side with the Archbishop of Toledo, rode young Alfonso. A battle took place, and although it lasted throughout one day it resulted in stalemate.

There was anarchy throughout the country and people were fighting one another on the slightest pretext, or perhaps no pretext at all. And on the 5th July, 1468, young Alfonso was discovered dead in his bed. The reason for his death remains a mystery; although we hear of certain trout of which he had partaken rather freely on the night before. Poison was naturally suspected and probably was used; although plague was raging at the time and may have been the cause of the young boy's death.

The death of her young brother brought a dramatic change in the life of Isabella for, since the legitimacy of La Beltraneja was in doubt she found herself in the direct line of succession. She was seventeen, and serious for her years; fully understanding the dangerous turmoil within the country and her own position with regard to it she very wisely retired to a nunnery at Avila, there to live in obscurity until it was safe for her to emerge.

She was visited at the nunnery by the Archbishop of Toledo who declared that he and his faction considered her to be the Queen of Castile on the death of her young brother Alfonso.

Isabella again showed her wisdom by declaring that she did not consider she had any right to the crown while her brother Henry lived. She also expressed doubts of heavenly approval, since Henry still lived and Alfonso had been the one to die. Her great desire, she added, was to see peace between the opposing factions, although she sincerely hoped that the licentious conduct of the court and the abuses which were carried on there, would be rectified.

As a result of Isabella's calm wisdom in the face of the glittering proposals which were laid before her, peace was restored on certain conditions. Henry was to divorce his Queen and send her back to Portugal; Isabella was to inherit the Asturias and become the heir of Castile and Leon; and she should not be forced to marry against her will, but at the same time she was not to enter into marriage without the consent of Henry.

Isabella was now a brilliant *partie* and was sought in marriage by many great personages, among them the brother of Edward IV of England, the Duke of Gloucester who was to become Richard III. There was also an offer from the brother of Louis XI (the Duke of Guienne). But Isabella had long dreamed of union between Aragon and Castile, and the suitor she favoured was Ferdinand of Aragon.

Chance seems to have played a great part in the lives of both Ferdinand and Isabella. At the time of their births it did not appear that they were destined to unite and rule Spain; yet in both cases all who stood between them and the crown were eliminated.

But for this marriage, but for the union of the states of Aragon and Castile, but for the piety of Isabella and the cupidity of Ferdinand, would the Inquisition have wilted away in Spain as it did in other countries? Had Henry been a strong man, had Alfonso not eaten trout or suffered from the plague, Isabella would have lived her life in comparative obscurity. And so easily Ferdinand might have done the same.

Yet they married; they became great rulers; they strengthened the Inquisition in Spain; and because of this thousands were to die the fiery death, thousands were to be humiliated and tortured. Isabella and Ferdinand united Spain; they drove the Moors from their last stronghold; it was under Isabella's aegis that Christopher Columbus discovered America; but all their achievements are darkened by the grim shadow of pain and death which they caused to be inflicted on so many people.

When Ferdinand came into the world, his father already had three children – Carlos, Blanche and Leonora – so his prospects were not very bright; perhaps this was why his ambitions were limitless.

In Aragon Alfonso V had followed his father, Ferdinand I, after the latter's brief reign; but Alfonso V spent little time in Aragon; he had conquered Naples and had set up his kingdom there, and finding the place to his liking, he appointed his brother John as Regent in Aragon.

John had married Blanche who was the daughter of Martin, King of Sicily; they had three children, all of whom lived tragic lives. The first was Carlos who was Prince of Viana; the second was Blanche who was the unfortunate wife of Henry of Castile and who was put aside by him in the humiliating manner already mentioned; and the third, Leonora, married Gaston de Foix. When John's wife Blanche died she left the kingdom of Navarre to her son Carlos (Blanche was the daughter of Charles III of Navarre) and according to the terms of her marriage contract this kingdom would, should her son die without heirs, pass to her other children even if they should be female.

John took a second wife. This was Joanna Henriquez who was a Castilian of royal blood, and the son she bore her husband was that Ferdinand who, with Isabella, was to rule Spain and foster the Inquisition in that unhappy land.

When Joanna's son was born she was obviously filled with ambitious longings to place him above his half brothers and sisters; and as she was a very strong-minded woman – and clearly a very clever one – she very soon set about gaining her desires.

The first thing she did was to set out for Navarre with the object of taking that kingdom from Carlos.

In Navarre there were two families of the Montague and Capulet type. These were the Beaumonts and the Agramonts. Their feud was of long standing and, if no one was quite sure what it was about, the enmity was not allowed to die away.

These two families seized every opportunity of taking sides against each other and, when Joanna showed her intention of taking Navarre from Carlos, the Beaumonts rose against her while the Agramonts took her side.

The Beaumonts surrounded the castle in which the Queen was staying and kept her besieged there. John came to her rescue, and the result was that as brother and brother fought against each other in Castile, so in Aragon the opponents were father and son.

The result of the battle was victory for John; and Carlos was taken prisoner.

John, under the influence of the strong-minded Joanna, was ready to be harsh with Carlos, while he doted on baby Ferdinand who at this time was only a few months old, having been born in March of that year, 1452.

Carlos was obviously a charming young man; he was gentle, and his manners were courteous. On being released – perhaps deploring the discord in his family and sensing the hatred which he, merely because he was his father's oldest son, inspired in his stepmother – he went to Naples to put himself under the care of his uncle Alfonso V in the hope that the powerful Alfonso would be able to bring about a reconciliation between him and his father.

Carlos was unfortunate, for Alfonso died, and when he did so John became King of Aragon, and an illegitimate son of Alfonso's (another Ferdinand) was left the Kingdom of Naples.

Carlos then went to Sicily which his father had inherited with Aragon, and there entered a monastery, such a life suiting his temperament.

The charm of Carlos was admired by the people of Sicily and the reports of his popularity reached John in Aragon. No doubt the Queen at his elbow, planning furiously for baby Ferdinand, was afraid that the Sicilians might elect Carlos as their ruler; and as Joanna had determined that her precious son should inherit his father's dominions, she wanted no sentimental preferences shown by any portion of those dominions, however small or remote.

It was not long before Carlos was recalled to Aragon. It was wrong for quarrels to persist in any family, John implied; and in royal families it was more than foolish; it was highly dangerous.

Carlos was advised by his Sicilian friends that he would be most unwise to return to Aragon; Carlos may have known this, but so gentle was his nature, and so did he abhor the friction in his family, that he decided to take a chance and return to his father.

It was now expected that John would name Carlos as his heir. Joanna, of course, was not going to allow this. Ferdinand was at this time eight years old – bright, intelligent, already aware of his mother's overpowering ambition on his behalf.

Joanna had so worked on the King that the only one of his children whose future seemed of real importance to him was Ferdinand.

Carlos now realized his folly in hoping to obtain a reconciliation with his father while John was under the influence of Joanna, who was determined to misconstrue all his actions and never lost the smallest opportunity of denigrating him for the advancement of her son.

Carlos looked about him for a way of escape, and asked for the hand of Isabella of Castile in marriage.

This enraged Joanna, for she had already been making plans for a marriage between Isabella and her own Ferdinand. It was acting under Joanna's advice that John had summoned his son Carlos to the Cortes; and when Carlos arrived he was arrested and put in prison.

The people of Aragon disliked the Queen and, like the Sicilians, they had been charmed by the personality and character of Carlos. There was an immediate reaction following the unfair imprisonment of Carlos, and a demand from the people to be told why John had imprisoned his son.

John's reply to this was that Carlos had plotted against his life, and he declared that even though he was his son, he should suffer the penalty for such an offence. As John had not yet left Lerida, the town in which the Cortes had taken place, the infuriated people rose in a body determined to make *him* their prisoner. However, he managed to escape, and the mob had the satisfaction of looting the palace in which he had been staying.

This, however, was the signal for revolution. The people of

Navarre rose in revolt against the King, and the Beaumont family, at the head of their followers, marched on Aragon.

Both John and Joanna were afraid, and both realized that it was the Queen in particular who had aroused the hatred of the people. Therefore, John, to save his face and to bring some favour back to the Queen at the same time, declared that he would release his son because his wife had implored him to do so. The Prince was released, and he was acclaimed with great affection by the people, who insisted that the King immediately accept him as his heir.

John had no alternative but to do this, and he complied with an air, not of resignation, but of pleasure as though the trouble had been the result of misunderstandings and it had always been his intention to do what now might seem to have been forced upon him.

Carlos, acclaimed, popular, now hoped to settle down to a life of peace among the people whose affection he had won. Unfortunately he was suddenly taken ill, and another of those mysterious deaths occurred at an opportune moment.

The Kingdom of Navarre now passed to Blanche, that sister of Carlos who had been repudiated by her husband, Henry IV of Castile. On the death of Blanche, Navarre would go to her father, and on his death to his daughter Leonora, the Countess of Foix.

Leonora and her family cast covetous eyes on Navarre. Her son Gaston had married a sister of Louis XI, King of France, and this son was very eager to rule Navarre; nor was the King of France averse to his possessing it, owing to Gaston's connection with the royal family.

Poor Blanche, who had suffered so much in Castile, now realized, as she considered the fate of her brother Carlos whom she had loved and supported wholeheartedly, that her life was in danger. She was very suspicious therefore when John suggested that she should go to France to stay with her sister Leonora because he believed it was possible to make a very good marriage for her there; he even suggested the King's brother, the Duc de Berri.

The terrified Blanche refused to go, but her father had her forcibly removed from her own estate; she was taken to her castle of Ortes in Béarn where, after two years, during which she was treated like a prisoner, in the care of Leonora and the Comte de Foix, terrified at the sound of every footstep, cautious of all she ate, she was poisoned.

It is gratifying to record that Leonora, who had caused her sister to be poisoned in order to obtain this kingdom, did not long enjoy it. When it eventually came to her after her father's death, Ferdinand was already stretching his greedy hands towards the family's possessions, and after Navarre had been but three weeks in the hands of Leonora, her half-brother seized it and Navarre became part of Ferdinand's kingdom.

Civil war continued to rage in Aragon, and the troubles of John came thick and fast in his old age. Leonora, impatient for his death, threatened to rise against him; and worst of all his eyesight began to fail him.

Queen Joanna emerges in all the vigour of her strong character at this time. She was determined to fight for the heritage of her son. She had made up her mind that Ferdinand should be king of Aragon and that his dominion should extend as far as she could possibly make it.

Accordingly she put herself at the head of the armies and, with the help of Ferdinand, prevented the utter defeat of King John.

But in the year 1468 she died and without her help the King was in despair. However, his luck seemed to change, for a Jewish doctor – miraculously it seemed at the time – operated on his eyes and saved his sight; and the Duke of Lorraine, who was his most formidable enemy and had put himself at the head of the Barcelonians, died suddenly leaving no heirs to lead the armies which had risen in revolt. So ended the civil war, with the King in possession of his kingdom and none to stand between Ferdinand and his inheritance.

Ferdinand was handsome and young – in fact a year younger than Isabella – and it was not only because of his future possessions that, of all the suitors who had been proposed, Isabella favoured Ferdinand.

Nevertheless there was great opposition to the match in Castile, and a faction, headed by Villena who was bitterly disappointed because the death of his brother prevented the family's connection with royalty, declared their support for La Beltraneja.

Henry, who had proclaimed Isabella as his heiress, was in a quandary and tried to marry La Beltraneja to Alfonso, the heir to the throne of Portugal.

He dared not explain his intentions, and as a blind the hand of Isabella was offered to Alfonso, son of the King of Portugal, who sent an embassy to Ocaña where Isabella was staying at that time. Isabella refused to consider the match, still determined on marrying Ferdinand of Aragon, and the people supported Isabella and made great efforts to show their support for the match by parading the streets with banners on which were displayed the combined arms of Aragon and Castile.

The King, however, abetted by Villena, was determined that Isabella should marry as they wished, and they continued to oppose the match with Aragon. Fortunately for Isabella war was raging in the south, and the presence of Henry and Villena was needed there; this gave Isabella her opportunity; she left Ocaña for Madrigal in the company of her mother, and they endeavoured to speed up the negotiations with Aragon concerning the marriage.

At Madrigal she found herself surrounded by the spies of Villena and her brother; and these men and women immediately began to bribe her personal servants to keep them informed of her actions that they might convey the news to Villena and her brother, Henry.

As a result Villena sent troops to Madrigal to secure Isabella, and make her a prisoner; however, the Admiral of Castile was Don Frederick Henriquez, who was the father of Ferdinand's mother and, since he saw the advantages to Ferdinand of a match with the heiress of Castile, he was ready to do all in his power to bring this about. The Archbishop of Toledo was also prepared to work for the marriage of Isabella and Ferdinand; and when these two men knew that troops were on the way to make Isabella a prisoner, they went with all speed to her palace and arranged for her to leave immediately. This she did, so that when the troops arrived they found she had escaped.

Isabella then came to Valladolid where the people turned out in their hundreds to greet her and to assure her that they were on her side.

Envoys were then despatched with all speed to Aragon that King John and Ferdinand might realize the difficult position of Isabella and speed up plans for the marriage.

John was at that time fighting for his kingdom against the Catalans, and consequently had no money to give Ferdinand for a wedding journey to Castile. It was arranged therefore that Ferdinand should enter Castile in disguise. His men would be dressed as merchants, and he as one of their servants. This ruse would not only excuse his arriving without the pomp and splendour expected; it was also necessary as there was so much opposition to the match from the King and Villena.

What chance at every turn attended this important union! Ferdinand might so easily have been killed before he was able to enter into it. On arriving at a castle where one of Isabella's adherents was waiting to give the party shelter, he and his friends were mistaken for enemies, and soldiers threw down great boulders from the battlements, one of which narrowly missed alighting on Ferdinand's head.

Isabella was delighted with her bridegroom. He was eighteen, fair and tanned by the weather; he excelled at sport; and Isabella must have recognized at once a strong man in this bridegroom of hers.

As for Isabella herself, we are told that she was very beautiful, although it is difficult to believe this when one studies her portraits. It may have been that she possessed those mild charms which, when accompanied by royal blood, are called, by contemporary courtiers, beauty. But at least she was young – nineteen years old; and Ferdinand, who had inherited his ambition from his mother would have seen, in addition to a very presentable young girl, the kingdom of Castile.

After that first meeting there was no need to wait – indeed it was unwise to wait. Neither party had enough money to pay for the wedding, so it was necessary to borrow, and this they did.

So, on the 19th October, 1469, in the palace of John de Vivero, where Isabella had been staying since her arrival in Valladolid, the marriage took place.

As soon as the ceremony was over the married couple sent an

announcement to Isabella's brother Henry, telling him the news.

Henry sent no congratulations; he replied merely that he would find it necessary to consult his ministers.

One result of the marriage was an immediate move by Villena and the King to make a match between Princess Joanna (La Beltraneja) and the Duke of Guinne (brother of Louis XI) who had been declined, in favour of Ferdinand, by Isabella.

Henry then issued a public proclamation that La Beltraneja was legitimate, and the Queen, her mother, joined him in swearing that the Princess Joanna was the daughter of Henry.

This made Isabella's hopes seem rather dark for, if the French marriage took place, La Beltraneja, on the death of Henry, would have the French supporting her claim to the throne.

During all these alarms Isabella remained calm, and her serenity made a great impression on all those who witnessed it; so much so that people began to hope that if Isabella continued as she had begun they could, under her rule, expect an end to the anarchy in which the kingdom had been plunged for so long and a return to sober living and piety.

The young couple lived in great poverty, relying on the generosity of their friends (who no doubt took the long view and looked upon this generosity as an insurance for the future).

Five dangerous years passed while the whole of Castile was plagued by the barbarous behaviour of its people. Robbery and murder were commonplace and amid all its attendant suffering the court pursued its licentious and most frivolous course.

Meanwhile Isabella lived a life of the utmost piety, serenely waiting.

In the December of 1473 there was a reconciliation between her and Henry who received her at his court and gave a series of fêtes in her honour. Unfortunately after a banquet Henry was taken ill, and it was not difficult for Isabella's enemies to suggest that there had been an attempt to poison him.

Henry's new friendship for his sister faded then, and he decided that she should become his prisoner, and once more his schemes were frustrated.

Villena died the following year, and Isabella no doubt believed that once his baleful influence was removed she might have a chance of again becoming friendly with her brother. This was not to be, for Henry, who had been suffering from an incurable disease for some time, himself died in December 1474.

The kingdom was weakened by civil wars, by the lack of administration and the anarchy which had been allowed to spread throughout the land.

There was scarcely any money in the treasury, and the state of the country had rarely been so low. There were two rivals for the throne, Henry's daughter (if she was his daughter) and his sister, Isabella.

To all appearances it seemed that the terrible wars which had ravaged the country during the last ill-fated reign would be continued in the years to come.

On the death of her brother, Isabella was proclaimed Queen. Ferdinand, who was at the time in Aragon, came hurrying to join her. They discussed the government and Ferdinand immediately stated his desire to take precedence over Isabella. Serene and peace-loving as Isabella undoubtedly was, she was also a woman who was determined to insist on her rights. Their adherents gathered about them and took sides; and after long discussions and arguments it was agreed that Isabella was the true heiress of Castile and Ferdinand must therefore derive his authority from her.

Ferdinand, chroniclers record, was somewhat piqued by this decision and haughtily declared that since he was of so little importance in Castile he would return to Aragon.

Isabella, however, was able to make him see reason and not show his petty pique at a time of their lives which might well be a very dangerous one. What did it matter in whose name the power was invested? They were husband and wife; their interests were similar. They had their daughter to think of. At this time they had only one child (called Isabella after her mother) who had been born in 1470 at Dueñas. Thus Isabella managed to soothe the wounded vanity of her young husband and keep him at her side in this most perilous time of their lives; and presumably Ferdinand learned wisdom, for in the future they worked together and, to show that they held equal authority, they made their device *Tanto monta, monta tanto – Isabel como Fernando*.

However they had difficulties to face before they were able to consolidate their kingdom; and Ferdinand had quickly to recover from his pique because it was not long before the supporters of La Beltraneja began to gather together and declare her to be the rightful heir to the throne. One of the chief of these was the Marquis of Villena, son of the old enemy, who was accounted to be one of the finest soldiers in the land. The Archbishop of Toledo, who had once stood so staunchly beside Isabella, treacherously joined her enemies. It was the old story of dissatisfaction with the power which had come his way. If he could not be Isabella's sole adviser, the Archbishop was ready to make a complete *volte-face* and be her enemy.

But there was one more powerful than either of these. This was Alfonso V of Portugal. Alfonso had several reasons for supporting the cause of La Beltraneja. The prospect of adding Castile to his dominions was inviting; moreover, Isabella had insulted him when she had shown so clearly her revulsion to marriage with him and her eagerness to marry Ferdinand.

Alfonso's idea was to take Castile and, in order to soothe the conquered Castilians, to marry La Beltraneja. There were two reasons which made this a little difficult; one was that the girl was only thirteen years old, but that could easily be ignored; the other was that she was his niece, her mother being Alfonso's sister. However, an obliging Pope would surely give the necessary dispensation to a monarch of Alfonso's importance. So, with this idea in view, Alfonso set forth to make war on Isabella and Ferdinand.

In May of 1475 he entered Castile, was welcomed by Villena and affianced to La Beltraneja, while a messenger was despatched to Rome for the dispensation. He and his bride-to-be were then declared the rightful sovereigns of Castile.

There then began the War of the Succession which was to last for four years, and in which Isabella and Ferdinand were eventually to be triumphant.

The Portuguese were decisively beaten near Toro, on that

occasion when the Portuguese standard-bearer, Edward de Almeyda, continued to hold the flag with his left hand after his right arm had been cut away, and held it in his teeth when he had lost both arms, until his body was hacked to pieces. But individual bravery could not win the battle for Alfonso, and his army was eventually in disordered retreat.

Alfonso himself so humiliated, declared his intention of going on a pilgrimage to the Holy Land and resigning his crown to his son John. However he was deterred from this project and advised to return to Portugal; which he did, arriving in time to prevent the coronation of John who gave up the crown to his father.

However, no sooner was Alfonso back on his throne than he began once more to cast envious eyes towards Castile and planned another expedition against Isabella. But Doña Beatriz of Portugal, who was an aunt of Isabella and sister-in-law to Alfonso, begged to be allowed to mediate and as a result she and Isabella met at the frontier and a treaty was drawn up.

This laid down that Alfonso should give up the arms with which he had invested himself as King of Castile and that he should break his engagement to La Beltraneja who should no longer claim the throne of Castile. She must either leave Portugal or agree to marry the son of Isabella and Ferdinand (Don John who had recently been born) or go into a convent. Alfonso, the Prince of Portugal, should be affianced to Isabella, the daughter of Isabella and Ferdinand.

This treaty was signed, and it put an end to the strife.

La Beltraneja, realizing that she had been deserted and doubting whether she would ever be allowed to marry the boy who was now but a baby, decided that she was tired of the world and would accept the alternative of a convent. She retired to Santa Clara of Coimbra where she took her vows.

Alfonso then declared that since he had lost his bride he would follow her example, for he too was tired of the world. He would enter the monastery of Varatojo. He died before he could carry out this intention.

Ferdinand's father had meanwhile died, and to Ferdinand fell the crown of Aragon.

Aragon and Castile were now as one state. The two sovereigns determined to unite Spain as she had never in her history been united. They determined to bring law and order into the land, so their thoughts naturally turned to the Kingdom of Granada.

Under Isabella and Ferdinand order was restored. They were determined to put an end to anarchy, and in this they were successful. Isabella had established the *Santa Hermandad* or the Holy Brotherhood which was in some respects a military force for protecting lives and property, and the *quadrilleros* (its officers) dealt with highway robbery, house-breaking, rape and other serious crimes. Taxes were levied on householders to maintain this service which proved to be efficient for, when a criminal was being hunted, bells were rung in those towns through which he was supposed to have passed and this resulted in many being brought to justice.

The laws were reformed; and after a few years the people were relieved of the great cost of the *Santa Hermandad*, for with the cessation of a great deal of the violence which had characterized the reign of Henry IV there was no longer need for such an elaborate institution; and in its place there was a police force to guard the safety of the people.

Naturally life was not all serenity; Isabella, as ruler of Castile, often had her difficulties to face; but it was quickly realized that the new respect for law and order was to the advantage of all worthy men and women and that they had good reason to be thankful for their Queen Isabella and her husband Ferdinand.

Isabella was seeing her plans materialize. She was becoming the Good Queen she had always wanted to be.

She was a woman of great piety; and it is said that she had once made a vow to her confessor, Tomás de Torquemada, that if she should come to the throne she would devote her life to the extirpation of heresy for the glory of God and the Catholic Faith.

Before Isabella had been many years on the throne there were those to remind her of this vow.

CHAPTER SIX

PERSECUTION OF THE JEWS

It is not possible to say when the Jews first came to Spain; they appear to have inhabited the country from earliest times. Ancient historians tell us that Japhet, one of the sons of Noah, was given Europe as his inheritance, and that his son Tubal and his adherents settled in Spain. Nebuchadnezzar II is reputed to have brought several tribes of Jews with him and settled in the peninsula. Consequently many synagogues were set up throughout the land and Judaism spread. St James came in A.D. 37 to instruct the Iberians in Christianity, to the consternation of the already large Jewish population.

Naturally enough on such a point there cannot be complete agreement between historians, and others tell us that the Jews did not arrive in Spain until after the Visigothic invasion.

It is inevitable that there has been disagreement between Jews and Christians: The Christians hating the Jews on account of the Crucifixion; the Jews contemptuous of a sect which had taken their old religion and grafted a new one on to it. They were natural enemies; but the Jews were ready to live side by side in peace with those whose opinions differed from their own; their great desires seemed to be to raise large families and become rich; the Christians, pioneers of a comparatively new religion, burned with the desire to convert.

The Jews, unfortunately for them, were a people who not only wished to make fortunes but to flaunt their wealth. They were lovers of flashing jewels and richly coloured garments. Had they lacked this love of ostentation they might have enjoyed a more peaceful existence. As it was, not only did they rouse the righteous indignation of Christians on account of the murder of Jesus Christ, but the envy of those Christians who were less successful. It may also have been that envy was a more dangerous emotion than righteous anger.

There had always been persecutions, but in the early centuries the persecutions were not severe and were generally confined to certain localities. As late as the reign of Alfonso VIII, who came to the throne in the year 1158, Jews were holding high positions at court; one was the King's treasurer, another his mistress. There appeared to be two types of Jew; the moneymaker, with his love of ostentation, and the intellectual who excelled in the arts, medicine, surgery and such professions. Both types had a great deal to offer the country they inhabited, and for a time the little irritations which the national character aroused could be forgotten.

But envy persisted and about the middle of the thirteenth century this envy grew into a menace against the Jews. Christians declared that the Jews made a mockery of the Crucifixion; and there was a rumour that a boy singer from Saragossa named Domingo de Val was kidnapped by Jews, who first whipped him, crowned him with thorns and then crucified him.

The Dominicans, ever ready to convert the peoples of the world to Christianity, had tolerance to spare those who remained outside their sphere. In the middle of the fourteenth century, when the Black Death swept over Europe with such devastating results, the Dominicans even blamed the Jews for that; and the people, whipped to fury against them by their own envy and the eloquence of the Dominicans, began to massacre them and rob them of their possessions. Taxes were levied against them, and Henry II who became King of Leon and Castile in 1369 demanded such large sums of them that it was often necessary for Jews to sell themselves into slavery to pay them as the only alternative to death.

This paved the way for the fanatic, Fernando Martinez. Martinez was a Dominican, and he was determined to arouse the violence of the people against the Jews. He confirmed the theory that the Jews were responsible for the Black Death; his reasons for this may have been the anger of Christ towards those who continually denied Him, or the habits of the Jews which were not considered to be as clean as those of Christians. For instance, they cooked their food with an abundance of oil and their persons were reputed to be maladorous. The first reason is more likely to carry weight than the second, for the people were more inclined to believe in the alleged cruel vindictiveness of Jesus Christ than in the virtue of cleanliness.

The preaching of Fernando Martinez resulted in pogroms in Catalonia, Aragon and Castile.

The Archbishop of Seville was appealed to by the terrified Jews, and the Archbishop, not insensible to the advantages brought to the country by the Jews, warned Martinez that he must desist.

Martinez however was a fanatic and therefore unafraid of the warnings of the Archbishop; and when the Pope, Boniface IX himself, added his voice to that of the Archbishop, still Martinez refused to stop his fulminations.

There were other occasions when Popes saw the folly of attacking the Jews. Clement VI, who took the Papal crown in 1342, intervened on their behalf when in Germany a choice between death and acceptance of the Christian Faith was offered them; and he even excommunicated those who attacked the Jews. Alexander VI, Roderigo Borgia, who reigned at the Vatican from 1492 to 1503, allowed them to live peaceably in Rome after they had been expelled from Spain. (It seems possible that the latter – a wily man always on the alert to seize an advantage, realized the affluence the persecuted race could bring to those lands in which they settled; and Alexander was almost as notorious for his love of wealth as for his scandalous personal life.)

Martinez, when reproached, declared that God put the words into his mouth and he personally had no power with which to thwart God's will even if he wished to.

The Archbishop of Seville, who naturally could not allow his authority and that of the Pope to be so flouted, brought Martinez for trial before an ecclesiastical court. An unfortunate incident happened at that stage. A few days before the examination of Martinez was due to take place, the Archbishop died.

The superstitious inclination of the people, always ready to read Divine interference in affairs of chance, led them to believe that the Archbishop had been struck dead by that vindictive monster whom they looked to in fear as their god, and that Martinez had really been speaking the truth when he said he merely uttered the words which had been put into his mouth.

Alas for the Jews! Martinez was awarded a position of high responsibility in the diocese, and no restraint was put upon his preaching.

Throughout Seville the riots started. Jews were robbed and murdered; their houses and synagogues put to the flames.

The Jews were ordered to live in their own quarters called *juderías* apart from Christians. This they did; but Martinez was not satisfied; he wanted blood as well as humiliation. The *juderías* or ghettos were attacked, and in Seville alone four thousand people were murdered.

Other towns, hearing of the excitement and realizing the richness of the spoils, were smitten with equal fervour to destroy those denied the divinity of Jesus Christ. The cry was: 'Baptism or Death.'

The numbers of the slain mounted to fifty thousand; and many Jews naturally chose to accept the Christian Faith in preference to a horrible death.

Those who were baptized were known as New Christians, *conversos*. More often though, the term *marranos* was applied to them as a form of abuse. Derived from the Hebrew *Maranatha* (The Lord is coming) is was said by the Christians to mean 'accursed'; and is now come to mean in Spanish 'sow'.

New decrees had been made against Jews. They were obliged to wear badges on their clothing in order that they might be immediately recognized as Jews; they were forbidden to shave or to ride on horseback; they must not be addressed as Don. They might not marry Christians nor indulge in sexual intercourse with Christians – even prostitutes – and if discovered doing any of these things suffered severe penalties. They were not allowed to hold any office in the state and were debarred from becoming innkeepers or apothecaries, surgeons or doctors.

But if they were baptized these restrictions were automatically lifted for the Jews as a race were not objected to; it was only their religion which gave offence. It is therefore not surprising that they accepted baptism in their tens of thousands.

Immediately they were released from the restrictions placed

upon them their resilience was phenomenal. In a few years' time the persecuted ones, fresh from the *juderia*, were becoming the wealthiest section of the population and, what is more amazing, finding their way into government posts. Some married into the nobility, for many noble families had become impoverished through periods of unrest in the country and were glad of the money which a Jewish marriage could bring. They even found their way into the Church.

The authorities might accept the *marranos*, but the masses murmured as they watched the growing prosperity of these people who, but a few years before had been shivering in the *juderia*.

The murmuring grew to a roar. Envy was abroad again, and the riots began. Now they were directed not towards the Jews who had remained Jews, but towards the new Christians who, declared the people, were Christians in name only and in the secrecy of their houses practised the rites of Judaism.

In 1449 when taxes were levied on the town of Toledo, it was discovered that many of the tax-collectors were Jews turned Christian. This incensed the people; and there was a rising against *marranos*.

Three years later a story was set in motion that a boy had been kidnapped and crucified at Valladolid. This was a rumour which appeared from time to time and could always be relied upon to inflame the people against Jews.

Two years after that, in 1454, there was another rumour. This concerned a Christian boy, kidnapped as the others had been, crucified, his heart cut from his body and burned.

Then in 1460 Alonso de Spina, a Franciscan, published a document in which he called attention to the wickedness of *conversos*. He was very violent, perhaps more so because he himself was a *converso*; perhaps he saw the growing anger of the people and was afraid that it would be turned on all *conversos* even if they should be holy Franciscans: he was determined to show that he was on the right side, by his venomous attacks on his own people. He made that demand – which was always flowing from the lips and pens of Dominicans and Franciscans: he wanted the Inquisition to be set up in Castile that it might deal adequately with these men and women who had outwardly accepted Christianity and secretly practised Judaism.

The Inquisition had not been established in Castile, although in 1474 Sixtus IV had ordered it to be introduced into Spain. As a result of this command Inquisitors had made their appearance in Catalonia, Valencia, Aragon and Navarre. Castile had remained outside the orbit of the organization as charges of heresy had been brought against so few people living there, and it had been decided that the bishops could deal adequately with these.

However Alonso de Spina thought otherwise. He assured his readers that Jews were the enemies of Christians; that they brought about the plague; that the reason people often fell into a mysterious illness because it was a Jewish custom to poison wells; and if previously they had doubted the rumours that it was a Jewish custom to kidnap boys and crucify them, as they had years ago crucified the founder of the Christian religion, they had only to recall the crucifixions of Valladolid and Zamora. These had been brought to light; how many more did they imagine had remained undiscovered?

He begged them to consider the Jews. They ate kosher food and cooked in oils. They ate too much, and consequently they stank. They were immoral and they had no respect for virginity; all they thought about was increasing the race.

Moreover they jeered at the holy rites of Christianity; and they had merely embraced the Faith for their material good. In secret they followed their own religion. They were guilty of the worst kind of heresy.

Not only did De Spina write; he set out on a tour which took him through Spain. Wherever he went he demanded action against the Jews and the introduction of the Inquisition into Castile to deal with them.

The Inquisition of course was a tribunal against heresy and could not deal with Jews unless they had become Christians, for only then could they be said to be guilty of heresy.

In 1468 there was another rumour of a crucifixion. On the Thursday of Holy Week, so the story goes, at Sepulveda a boy was kidnapped, crowned with thorns, whipped and crucified. This time there was an enquiry, and the result was that a party of men were arrested, found guilty and condemned to death.

Whether there were Jewish communities who were guilty of this ritual murder it is difficult to say. It may have been that these crucifixions actually took place. Jews had suffered a great deal from the hands of Christians; they may have used this cruel method of retaliation.

However, popular opinion was becoming so inflamed that it was obvious that some action against the *marranos* was inevitable.

Isabella was not eager to establish the Inquisition on Castilian soil, and had made it clear from the beginning of her reign that she – not even Ferdinand – was ruler of Castile. Isabella's reasons were that she had no wish to put herself under the influence of Rome.

The reigning Pope was Sixtus IV, and Isabella had already been involved in a disagreement with him.

Sixtus had been elected to the Papal chair in 1471. He was the son of a fisherman, and it has been said that he never could adjust himself to the splendour of the Vatican; extremely clever – he must have been to have risen so high from such humble beginnings – he was an excellent administrator; he was however noted for that besetting sin of medieval Popes: nepotism. He lost no time in making sure that all relations and friends were well set up in life, and this brought him occasional difficulties.

Isabella had asked that her chaplain, Alsonso de Burgos, be given the bishopric of Cuenca which had fallen vacant. Sixtus would have been pleased to grant her wish, but it so happened that his nephew Raffaele Riario, Cardinal of Sen Sisto, had cast acquisitive eyes on Cuenca. Naturally the post went to the nephew of Sixtus.

Isabella and Ferdinand were very angry. As a matter of fact it was not the first time their suggestions had been ignored, for when Isabella had sought the Bishopric of Tarragona and the Archbishopric of Saragossa for two of her protéges, the Pope had been unable to grant her wishes, because he had two dear friends on whom he wished to bestow these benefices.

To be set aside on three occasions was more than Ferdinand

and Isabella could be expected to endure; they therefore asked the Pope (first gently and then less gently) to cancel the appointment he had given to his nephew and bestow it on Alonso de Burgos.

This sent up the Papal eyebrows. Sixtus explained, with as much patience as he could muster at such an affront to his dignity, that God had given him his power and none but God could take it from him.

Not for the first time in the history of Rome there was coldness between reigning Pope and sovereigns. Isabella and Ferdinand recalled their ambassador from the Vatican and ordered Spanish subjects to leave Rome.

This was not all. Ferdinand and Isabella informed the Pope that they proposed to call a council that the powers of the Papacy might be discussed, and Sixtus, knowing that there had been considerable dissatisfaction throughout Rome on account of his flagrant nepotism, could not face the findings of such a council.

He therefore – wise man that he undoubtedly was – humbled himself, withdrew the nominations, not only from his own nephew but from the other two which had brought him into conflict with the Spanish rulers, and bestowed those honours on the candidates nominated by Ferdinand and Isabella.

This was a great victory for Ferdinand and Isabella, and particularly for Isabella as, in matters appertaining to Castile, she always took the lead; and she was firm in her decision that she would not allow the Vatican to encroach on her domain.

There were many people about the throne to urge the introduction of the Inquisition. Isabella, aware of Papal influence among the clergy, was wary; but there was one person whom she trusted. This was Tomás de Torquemada, who had been her confessor.

Isabella listened to him but, still afraid of the infiltration of too much Papal influence, turned again and again from the suggestion of bringing the Inquisitors into Castile.

Alonso de Ojeda the Prior of the Dominicans of Seville, was a zealous fanatic, and he sought an audience with the Queen, for Ferdinand had left for Estremadura to review the fortifications on the frontiers of Portugal. With great fervour

Ojeda pointed out to Isabella that she must put a stop to the spread of Judaism. Hs assured her that the only way to do this effectively was to establish the Inquisition.

The Queen listened in her gentle, courteous manner; she herself had established several *conversos* in her entourage and was fond of them; she was fully aware that the outcry against the *marranos* was very often caused by envy of their possessions. Isabella sincerely wished to maintain justice in Castile. She had received a poem written by a *converso* in which he vividly described the terrible injustice which was so often the lot of his fellows, and she had been deeply moved by the poem and the sufferings of this section of her subjects.

She was supported in her attitude by Don Pedro Gonzalez de Mendoza who was the Cardinal of Spain and Archbishop of Seville. He appears to have been a humane man. He was an aristocrat and lover of luxury; he wished to live comfortably himself and liked to see others do the same. He had entered the Church, not perhaps so much because he had a vocation for it, but because through the Church he saw a means of living the intellectual life of a nobleman. Besides being a priest he was a writer and enjoyed translating Latin verse. Such a man lacked all the zeal of men like St Dominic, St Francis and Torquemada, but made life much more comfortable and pleasant for his fellows than did these zealous men.

The Archbishop had no desire to see the Inquisition installed in Castile; and strongly he advised Isabella against allowing its entry. The Queen accepted the Archbishop's advice, much to the chagrin of Ojeda.

At this time there arrived in Spain the chief Inquisitor of Sicily: Filippo de' Barberi. He added his voice to Ojeda's; and when they both realized that it was almost impossible to convince Isabella, they determined to work on Ferdinand.

Ferdinand lacked the finer qualities of his wife. He was a man of deep sensual desires and he had never seriously sought to restrain these. He was anxious however to prove himself a true follower of the Faith, and any way of doing this which did not interfere with his pleasures was agreeable to him. There was one characteristic which he possessed to a large degree; this was acquisitiveness. It may have been that his mother, when she had fought so hard to make him his father's heir, had inbued him with the cupidity and love of self-aggrandizement which he possessed. However it became clear to those whose desire it was to install the Inquisition in Spain that it was this cupidity of Ferdinand's which must be played upon.

Isabella was still determined to be mistress in her own kingdom and no matter who attempted to influence her – even Ferdinand himself – it must be she who had the last word.

Pious as she was, determined to see Christianity firmly established, she called to her the Archbishop of Seville and commanded him to prevent the spread of Judaizing among *conversos*.

This move incensed those who had been working to establish the Inquisition, for they were aware of the leniency of the Archbishop and they felt that all their work, all their importuning, had brought them nowhere.

The Archbishop applied assiduously to his task, compiled an *instruccien* in a manner of a catechism, and this was taught in schools and by priests in the churches.

There the matter might have rested for some time. Isabella was satisfied that she had done her duty by placing the correction in the hands of the Archbishop whom she knew to be a just man. But a certain incident occurred; this, though trivial in itself, was to change the situation and make the way for the introduction of the Inquisition into Castile.

A young man, said to be of the noble house of Guzman, had a mistress who belonged to a *converso* family. It was this young man's custom to visit the girl in her father's house in the *judería*. These visits were secret from the girl's family who doubtless would have frowned on her receiving a lover in her rooms.

The young man was paying one of these visits to the girl on March 18th in the year 1478. This happened to be Holy Week; it was also the eve of the Jewish Passover which, of course, was celebrated for eight days in April. During his love-making the Guzman grew uneasy when he became aware of comings and going below and evidence of excitement in the house.

The girl, terrified that she and her lover would be discovered, led him quietly downstairs, hoping to let him out of the house. She was frustrated in this by the sound of voices and presumably shut him into a cupboard or in some place where he was concealed.

While the young man was waiting to make his escape, the girl's father and her friends came and stood close to his place of concealment and the Guzman heard their conversation.

He understood that they, who were supposed to be New Christians, were in reality assembled together to celebrate the Passover.

The young man was horrified. It is extraordinary that these people, who were merely practising their own religion after having been forced to adopt another, should seem to him to be committing a major sin, whereas he himself, having entered this man's house in order to seduce his daughter and being forced to hide in an undignified manner for fear of discovery, would seem to be committing a minor one.

This attitude was typical of the times. And this young man, in spite of the fact that he had professed to be in love with the daughter of the house, lost no time, after making his escape, in informing against her family.

Ojeda, to whom he went with the story, was delighted; and as a result those who had assembled at the home of the Guzman's mistress were arrested.

Confessions were made, and the offenders implored that their sins might be forgiven and they themselves restored to the Church.

Fortunately for them the Inquisition had not been introduced into Castile, and their request was granted, after a penance had been performed.

Ojeda made all haste to Cordova where Isabella had been joined by Ferdinand.

But before seeking an audience with them he obtained one with Tomás de Torquemada and told him the story of the lovers and the *conversos* who had been practising Judaism in secret. Torquemada, deeply shocked – not by the behaviour of the Guzman but that of the *conversos* – went with Ojeda into the presence of their sovereigns and joined his pleading with that of Ojeda, assuring them that for the glory of the Catholic Church and the good of Spain the Inquisition must be introduced without further delay.

Ferdinand, visualizing the financial gain which could ensue from the establishment of the Inquisition, and weighing this against the probable strengthening of Papal influence, was eventually won over. Isabella followed her husband, but reluctantly, and at last they asked Sixtus IV to allow them to set up the Inquisition in Castile.

Sixtus granted their request in November, 1478. Yet, although the sovereigns had obtained this permission, they made no use of it for two years.

There is a difference of opinion as to why Isabella was so dilatory in making use of the Inquisition. Catholic historians tell us that she was a pious woman, reluctant to bring suffering to her subjects, eager to give those who offended against the laws of the Catholic Church an opportunity to repent. Her reluctance to set up the Inquisition is pronounced to be due to these qualities. There is however another opinion, which is that Isabella was determined to establish Catholicism throughout her country and was in complete agreement with the methods used by Tomás de Torquemada; and that the reason for the delay had nothing to do with the delicacy of her feelings but was due to a disagreement with the Pope – Isabella demanding that the Inquisition should be appointed by the sovereigns of Spain, that the confiscated goods of heretics should be their concern only, and that Rome should have no voice in the disposal of such property.

It would seem that neither of these opinions is clear cut. Since the Bull of 1478 gave Isabella and Ferdinand what they asked, this would explain the delay in setting up the Inquisition in the first place; and Isabella was undoubtedly endowed with the gifts of Statescraft. On the other hand, when the Bull was in her possession and all her conditions were granted, still there was two years delay before she took extreme measures.

Isabella, I believe, wanted peace in her country; she had learned a great deal from the disastrous rule of her father and brother. She was determined to make her country uniformly

Catholic, but it does appear that she would have preferred to do this without cruelty.

Moreover when the Bull was received from the Pope, Torquemada had returned to his convent and Cardinal Mendoza was with the Queen, no doubt urging her to continue with the methods he had put into force.

Torquemada at this time was dealing with the affairs of Hernan Nuñez Arnalt who had left a great deal of money for the founding of a monastery at Avila; he had assigned to Torquemada the right to supervise all the necessary arrangements, and this project, very dear to the heart of Torquemada, absorbed him, even to the exclusion of the persecution of heretics.

Both sovereigns were very busy with political matters, for Ferdinand had only that year taken the crown of Aragon; but in the spring of 1480 Isabella and Ferdinand went to Toledo where the Cortes had assembled. The object of this visit was to accept the oath of allegiance to Isabella's little son, Juan, the Prince of the Asturias, who was nearly two years old.

During the Cortes, the old laws regarding *marranos* were discussed, and it was agreed that these had been allowed to lapse. Thereupon it was decided that they should be enforced once more; that all Jews should not be seen abroad without the red badge on their shoulders; that they should not emerge from their *juderias* after dusk, and that none of them should enter a profession which had been denied to them.

Catholic historians declare that this is yet another example of Isabella's reluctance to introduce the Inquisition, another attempt to banish heresy through humane methods.

The Jews, who had been gradually emerging once more from their bondage, were very bitter at being thrust back, and one of them was misguided enough to write a pamphlet, and even more misguided to publish it. Unfortunately in expressing himself with great fervour he had fallen into heresy, and this was pointed out by Hernando de Talavera the monk who was later to become Archbishop of Granada.

The publication of this pamphlet is said to have destroyed the last of the Queen's patience. It is also said that Ferdinand, thinking of the rich possessions of heretics which would fall to the state, was urging her to take action. The fact is that in

September of that year (1480) Isabella commanded Cardinal Mendoza and Tomás de Torquemada to nominate Inquisitors; and as there was reputed to be more heresy rampant in the town of Seville than in any other, the Dominicans, Miguel Morillo and Juan de San Martino, were appointed Inquisitors.

In October, Ferdinand and Isabella issued a command that it was the duty of all citizens to make the work of Inquisitors easy by giving them all the help they needed.

The Inquisition arrived in Seville in a procession. The Inquisitors, in their white robes and black hoods, accompanied by friars and familiars, must have struck a note of awe and terror in all who beheld them. The Dominicans, after their custom, were barefoot and their robes were coarse; at the head of the procession marched a Dominican monk carrying the cross. Through the streets they walked on their way to the Convent of St Paul where they would begin their hideous work. The people, we are told, watched them in silence and – most certainly – apprehension. There was good reason for this.

Meanwhile many of the *conversos* had made their escape from Seville and taken refuge on the estates of certain great nobles, such as the Duke of Medina Sidonia, who they believed would give them protection.

This they were to discover was a foolish action to have taken. If, the officers of the Inquisition declared, people felt it necessary to escape, they must be guilty. Suspicion was aroused in the Inquisitorial breast; this was a shadow of things to come, suspicion being often all that the Inquisition needed to condemn.

Commands were sent to the Duke of Medina Sidonia, the Marquis of Cadiz and others who had given shelter to the *conversos*. The Inquisitors must be supplied with the names of all those who had fled to them for shelter; moreover these people must be arrested and brought to the offices of the Inquisition for questioning. Anyone who did not obey the wishes of the Inquisitors would himself be immediately suspected of heresy; for was it not an offence against Holy Church to harbour heretics? The dreaded threat of excommunication was mentioned.

So, very soon after the dreary procession had passed through the streets of Seville, the prisons of the Inquisition were filled and the bloody work was about to begin.

It was very difficult for some people who had been living in Seville to realize what was happening. The rules had been lax for some time, and it was easy to forget the years of persecution when a period of comparative ease had been enjoyed.

Some of the *marranos* of Seville had prospered and, as was the habit of their race, given a few years of peace, had become rich.

There was one man living in Seville who was reputed to be possessed of great wealth – ten million *maravedis*. He was Diego de Susan, a man of great importance in the town; he had also been to the fore in municipal matters, and when he saw the grim procession parading the streets, it did not occur to him that those pale hard-faced men with their monks' robes and bare feet could not be prevented from changing the way of life in Seville.

Therefore he called together other important men of the town, and in his house there took place a meeting during which measures were discussed to turn out these intruders, that the life of Seville might go on in the pleasant, prosperous way of the past.

Diego de Susan reminded his friends that they themselves were doing no harm to anyone; that they were popular in the town, for the people realized they made it prosperous; they were rich; they had many servants; if they stood together they could fight the Inquisitors and make it impossible for them to remain in Seville.

He was evidently a man of forceful personality, for he drew many prominent men into his scheme; moreover he convinced them that they, with their men and money could overcome the monks and turn the Inquisition out of Seville.

They might easily have done so, but luck was against them.

Diego de Susan had a daughter. She was so beautiful that she was known throughout Seville as *la hermosa hembra.* This girl had a Christian lover, and to him she betrayed the conspiracy.

No one knows why the girl behaved thus. Some say she did it

in a moment of weakness; others that she was pregnant, and therefore unaccountable for her actions. The fact remains that the conspirators were betrayed, and by the daughter of the chief of them.

Nothing could have given the Inquisitors more pleasure. They had an excuse to arrest all the principal citizens of Seville on suspicion. These men were taken to the Convent of St Paul for questioning, and there were tried on a charge of heresy.

Six of them were found guilty, and the citizens of Seville experienced the horror of watching the grim procession through the streets. This was not to be compared with the horrific pomp which was to be a feature of the *autos de fé* of the future.

The six were compelled to wear the horrible yellow garment of shame, and carry lighted candles in their hands; halberdiers marched beside them to prevent any attempt, on their part, to escape, or among the spectators to rescue them. At the head of the procession walked a Dominican, with coarse robe and bare feet, holding the banner of the Inquisition; he was followed by the familiars of the institution walking in pairs; after them were the condemned men and the guards, followed by the Inquisitors and a party of Dominicans led by Alonso de Ojeda.

From the convent to the Cathedral went the procession, there to halt for Mass and a sermon by Ojada. Garcia Roderigo, that firm defender of the Inquisition, declares that Ojada had done all in his power to urge the men to reform, as he hoped to save them. But as these men had in reality been arrested and condemned, not for their lack of faith, but for their conspiracy against the installation of the Inquisition in Seville, this can scarcely be believed.

Eventually the procession left the Cathedral for the fields of Tablada, and there the first *auto de fé* of Castile took place.

Even Andérs Bernaldez, a stern upholder of the Inquisition, does not deny that Diego de Susan met his death as a brave man and a Christian; and if he is right and Susan died in the Christian Faith, nonsense is made of Garcia Roderigo's statement that Ojada laboured long to save him from the fiery death. In any case such labours do not fit in with what we know of Ojeda.

This *auto de fé* took place on 6th February 1481. It was the first of many.

As for La Susanna, *la hermosa hembra*, legend has it that she was overcome with remorse when she realized what she had done, and that the Bishop of Tiberiades arranged that she should be given shelter in a convent and there take the veil. The girl, however, was unable to settle down to convent life and, escaping from it, became a prostitute. In the course of this profession she bore several children, and when her beauty was lost and the nobility were no longer interested in her she found a home with a humble grocer. By the time of her death the daughter of the millionaire of Seville was in abject poverty; and as she lay dying she asked that her skull should be placed over the doorway of that house where she had lived whilst pursuing her immoral life.

This was meant to be an example to all of the fate which had overtaken her, whether on account of the evil life she led or because of the great betrayal, one is not quite sure. There grew of course the usual legends surrounding the skull, and there were many to declare that they had heard cries of remorse coming from it in the dead of night.

The skull remained there however for centuries, and the story has been remembered – if not because of La Susanna – because her father was the man who tried to stage a rising against the Inquisition and consequently became one of its first victims in Seville.

The sight of those human bodies writhing in the flames, the sound of their groans, inspired the Inquisitors to greater efforts. They wanted more burnings, more human sacrifices.

Ojeda was urging the people of Seville to provide him with heretics; if they did not produce them, they themselves would very soon come under suspicion, for heretics he must have. At this time however the plague which had been raging through Spain came to Seville, and in the streets men, women and children who had been struck down were unable to reach their homes and lay dying. One of the first victims was Ojeda himself. He was dead within a few days. He had witnessed the first *auto de fé* and had planned many, much more impressive, to follow; but the first was his last; and with the plague came a respite for Seville, for it was impossible to carry on the work of the Inquisition in such a stricken city, and it became necessary for the Inquisitors to move out of the town. They set up their headquarters temporarily at the village of Aracena. Alas for Aracena! The zealous Dominicans could not rest from their labours, and the result of their sojourn in that village was an *auto de fé* for which they managed to find twenty-three victims.

The plague in Seville was replaced by a worse enemy; the Inquisition returned. Now a state of terror reigned in the town. It had been seen how useless it was to protest. There was the example of Diego de Susan who had been one of the town's most powerful men. *Autos de fé* were now being held at the rate of about one a month, and the Inquisitors were indefatigable in their search for victims. The dungeons of the convent were full and no more could be kept there; many were taken to the Castle of Triana close to the city. There were vast dungeons in the castle, but these too were very soon filled to their capacity.

Not content with burning the living, the Inquisitors brought charges of heresy and apostasy against the dead whose bodies were dug up and publicly burned.

Victims were needed so new edicts were issued. All those who were guilty of heresy or apostasy were urged to come forward and confess. A time limit was given for them to do this; if any failed to do so and were discovered in their sin they would, they were warned, meet with little mercy.

Twenty thousand *conversos* came forward, trembling with terror, to admit that had at times practised Jewish rites.

Confession must be sincere, was the answer to these poor people; and their sincerity could only be credited if they informed against those of their acquaintances who had been equally guilty.

The twenty thousand were faced with two alternatives. If they did not name some they suspected were guilty, their own repentance could not be relied upon; therefore it was the stake for them and ignominy and poverty for their children, because of the law of the Inquisition was, as they knew, confiscation of property. On the other hand if they betrayed others their repentance would be accepted.

These poor people were in a terrible dilemma. It is true that many betrayed their friends. Thus were many human sacrifices provided for the fire, which, says a Catholic recorder who was also a priest (Andérs Bernaldez), was a glorious affair, for not only were these sinners brought back to the Church but they exposed those more guilty men and women who had not answered the call to repent.

Those fiends, Morillo and San Martino (against whose cruelty even the Pope protested) then issued a second edict. In this it was commanded that every citizen must search for those practising Judaism in their midst and, if they were *conversos*, the attention of the Inquisition must be called to them. Any failing to do his duty was himself in danger of being accused of heresy and must be prepared not only for excommunication but examination by the Inquisitors.

It would be no use their declaring innocence of the vile practises in which Jews indulged. To prevent this a list of all Jewish rites was to be published that all might know for what they had to look.

The whole of the population was panic-stricken: the Jews who were almost all *conversos* (for it had been necessary to receive baptism in order to live in Spain), and the Christians who could be accused of knowing that Jewish rites were practised, yet failing to report this.

The people must listen to the conversation about them, and if they heard any man, woman or child say that they were waiting for the coming of the Messiah, then that person did not believe that the Messiah had already came and had thereby committed an offence against Christianity. He must be reported at once to the Inquisition.

Naturally any who they knew had returned to Judaism after baptism must be reported. But this was a matter which all guilty of such sin would keep to themselves, so it would be necessary for those who wished to be considered good Christians to be very alert. They must watch for any who kept the Jewish Sabbath: Did they light no fires in their houses on Friday night and remain in their homes, doing no work? Did they put on clean clothing?

The manner in which they slaughtered animals for their food must be observed. Did they cut the throats of the animals including poultry and bleed them? Did they eat meat in Lent? Did they celebrate the Jewish feasts and fasts? They would of course do this in secret but it was the duty of all good men of the Church to detect them. Did they bless their children by laying hands on their heads without making the sign of the Cross? The law of Moses declared that women should not enter churches for forty days after bearing children. Let the Christians watch for those who respected this law. Let them report any child which had been circumcised or given a Hebrew name. Let them watch for any who took the *Ruaya*, that ceremonial supper before starting on a journey. If in any house a person died with his face turned to the wall, or had had his face turned to the wall by any person at his death-bed, then that house was suspect. If a corpse was washed and shaved and dressed for the tomb, if water was sprayed in houses of the dead, if while mourning there was abstention from the eating of meat, then those who behaved in this way were suspect, because this was in compliance with the Mosaic law.

No one who had been a Jew and become a Christian was safe. The historian, Juan Antonio Llorente, declares that the Inquisitors were determined to condemn thousands in the town of Seville because they wished to show the Queen how rife was heresy in that town, so that she, who had been so reluctant to establish the Inquisition should recognize the need for it.

Llorente was clearly a man of great integrity, and Rafael Sabatini, who quotes him frequently in his *Torquemada and the Spanish Inquisition*, writes that he is an historian of 'unimpugned honesty and authority'. He also gives a brief biography of this extraordinary man, to the effect that he was born at Logroño in 1756 and twenty-three years later was an ordained priest, after taking a University course in Roman and Canon law. These qualifications brought him a seat on the Supreme Council of Seville, which was of course the Council of the Inquisition. He became the Commissary of the Holy Office in his birth-place, when it was necessary to give definite proof that he had no Jewish or Moorish blood in his veins.

He was a man of an enquiring mind however, a man who

determined to think for himself – a quality likely to be frowned upon in the circles in which he moved. As a result of these ideas of his he was sent to a monastery to do a penance; and it was necessary for him to find a new occupation.

When Napoleon came to Spain and the Inquisition was abolished (temporarily) Llorente had an opportunity of going through the massive archives of the Institution.

He was eventually expelled from Spain, and while in Paris he wrote his book *Historia Critica de la Inquisicion de España*.

No one could have been better equipped to write such a book, and naturally enough he was reviled both by the Spanish Government and the Church. He was unfrocked and forbidden to teach in schools. However, disgraced in the eyes of the Church though he might be, before he died at the age of sixty-six he had given the world valuable information concerning the crimes of the Inquisition; and given it in a manner which inspired confidence – as the excuses for and glorification of the Holy Office by such writers as Garcia Roderigo on the Catholic side, and the venomous attacks on it by William Harris Rule, D.D. on the Protestant side, could not do.

What an unhappy city Seville must have been at this time with the dismal incantations of the monks which filled the streets during the hideous processions, and smell of the burning flesh of martyrs, and perhaps worst of all that atmosphere of suspicion, the feeling that no one was safe from friend, neighbour or even family. Children were encouraged to inform against parents, husbands against wives, wives against husbands. A similar situation existed and still exists, we know in some countries in this twentieth century. Repellent as this practice must always be, to spy and to incriminate falsely for the State seems less culpable than to do so in the name of Christ. The first is unnatural and shocking; so is the second, but when added to the unhealthy qualities there is hypocrisy and the hope of salvation in the world to come, the shame is surely doubled.

None was more assiduous in discovering heretics than the friars. There is the case of the friar who early on Saturday mornings climbed onto the roof of the Convent of St Paul's to make a note of those houses from whose chimneys no smoke was rising.

Smokeless chimneys meant no fire. Who were these people who had omitted to light a fire on a Saturday? Surely they must be *conversos* who had reverted to Judaism.

A smokeless chimney was enough to drag a man or woman before the Inquisitors; and once in their hands it was a short step to the torture chamber and the stake.

The first *auto de fé*, on 6th February, when Susan and his friends had perished, was speedily followed by another, on March 26th and before the end of the year – Llorente tells us, and he should know, having access to the archives – 298 people had been burned alive in the town of Seville alone, and 79, repenting in time, were sent to life-long imprisonment. Many corpses of dead suspects were dug up and given public burnings, all of which took place on the meadows of Tablada where a stone platform had been built. This spot was called the *Quemadero*, the Burning Place.

Many of the *conversos* had managed to escape from Spain, and some of them had actually gone to Rome to protest to Sixtus IV. They assured him that they were good Christians but that in spite of this they were unsafe in Seville where one's enemies only had to make a lying statement to the authorities for a man or woman to have no chance of redress.

Sixtus, who in any case was displeased with Isabella and Ferdinand on account of the conditions they had forced him to accept at the time when the Inquisition was established in Castile, declared that the Inquisitors were not behaving in accordance with the rules laid down by the Inquisition, and he sent a protest to the two sovereigns. They themselves he pointed out, had wished to appoint the Inquisitors, and it appeared that the two who had been appointed were not satisfactory. He therefore withdrew the permission he had given them to elect their own Inquisitors, and declared that, should he receive more complaints, he would make use of his powers to remove from those posts these men nominated by the two sovereigns.

Isabella and Ferdinand made no protest. It may have been that the appointing of Inquisitors did not concern them so deeply as that other concession which they had wrung from Sixtus: that which gave the two sovereigns the right to take the confiscated goods of the condemned.

Was it coincidence that so many of the condemned people had been very rich? Ferdinand's eyes must have glistened with joy when he saw the money which was being provided to equip the army he wanted to lead against the Moors of Granada. Isabella's very likely glistened also, even though she might have pressed her palms together and knelt in prayer asking the saints to intercede for Christ's help in giving her an all-Catholic kingdom.

Sixtus then appointed eight Dominicans as a council to direct the affairs of the Inquisition; at their head was Alonso de Cebrian, and among them was Tomás de Torquemada.

At the Pope's decree a court of appeal was set up in Spain; and Bulls were prepared that they might be sent to the Archbishops, reminding them that the utmost integrity must be employed within the Inquisition; but when refugees continued to arrive in Rome with their complaints, the Pope decreed that any man or woman who was ready to be reconciled to the Church should be given the chance to be so.

Sixtus however did not send these Bulls. He withheld them to reconsider certain points; and unfortunately for thousands, they were never despatched.

Isabella and Ferdinand, realizing that the Inquisition had grown to be the most powerful force in Spain and that it was partly governed by Rome, implored Sixtus to put a man at its head who could stabilize it and control those who displeased the Pope.

They had a suggestion to make as to who could best fill this role. The Pope concurred with their selection and Tomás de Torquemada was appointed to preside over the Supreme Council of the Inquisition (the Suprema).

On 2nd October, 1483, Torquemada was made Inquisitor-General for Castile, and fifteen days later Aragon was joined with Castile under his jurisdiction.

CHAPTER SEVEN

TORQUEMADA AND HIS 'INSTRUCTIONS'

No name has been more closely connected with the Spanish Inquisition than that of Tomás de Torquemada, and there must be few people who have never heard of it. It is strange that this man, who for the first fifty-eight years of his life lived in comparative obscurity, should in his remaining twenty years have left such a mark on the world; and it is characteristic of human judgment that in some that name should arouse horror and in others admiration, in some disgust and in others something like adoration. Tomás de Torquemada has been called a cruel bigot; he has also been called the light of Spain, the saviour of his country and the honour of his Order.

Tomás was born in the year 1420 in a small town close to Valladolid; and the name of that small town was, of course, Torquemada. And how apt it proved to be!

He came of a good stock; they were petty nobles; the family having received its distinction in the fourteenth century under Alfonso XI when he had knighted Lope Alonso de Torquemada.

Tomás's uncle, Juan de Torquemada, was the famous theologian and writer. Juan had delighted the Vatican by his firm defence of Papal infallibility, and his reward had been the bestowal of the purple and the office of Cardinal of San Sisto.

The great Cardinal's brother was Pero Fernandez; Tomás was the latter's son.

From his early childhood Tomás showed his bent, and his love of piety of the most austere type was remarkable. He was very studious, distinguished himself as a scholar, and at a very early age received his doctor's degree in divinity and philosophy.

He was however aware of a vocation and after this brilliant

scholastic career he made it clear to his family that he wished to enter the order of the Dominicans.

This must surely have been a blow to Pero Fernandez, for Tomás was an only son and the family must have hoped he would marry and continue the line. However, so firm was Tomás's determination that, young as he was, he entered the Order and was given the appointment of Prior in the Monastery of Santa Cruz at Segovia.

From the beginning Tomás showed his austere nature, submitting himself to all possible hardship, refusing to eat meat at all and living on a meagre diet; he refused to wear linen next his skin and this must have been a great discomfort, for the Dominican habit was of very coarse material. To make himself more uncomfortable still he often wore a hair shirt. He went bare-foot, and many marvelled at the humility of this nobleman who chose the life of a humble friar.

The news of his piety spread and, when Isabella was brought under the care of her brother Henry IV, it was Tomás de Torquemada for whom she asked, to be her confessor.

This was not seen at that time to be the post of importance which it turned out to be, for Isabella was then merely the King's sister and there appeared to be little likelihood of her reaching the throne.

There is however a story which is probably false and which may have been concocted afterwards in the light of what followed: Torquemada, while Isabella's confessor, is reputed to have extracted a promise from her that if ever she became Queen she would bring back the Inquisition to Spain.

Of course she did bring it back, and one of the people who had urged her to this course and who helped to strengthen it and make it the dreaded thing it became was Tomás de Torquemada. In any case Isabella had the highest possible opinion of her confessor and it was to him she turned again and again for advice.

During the time he spent with Isabella as her confessor Torquemada undoubtedly won her confidence, for when she became Queen she made him one of her most trusted advisers.

There seems to be little doubt that Torquemada was sincere. He was not, as so many of the Church, a seeker after wealth, and if he wanted power he appears to have won it in order to establish the Catholic Faith throughout the land. He wanted to force all men to share the austerity which he himself was prepared to practise. To some of us today his confidence that he and he alone was right smacks of a conceit so great that it belongs to that Pride included in the deadly sins. However there were many – and still are many – who construe this trait as a virtue bordering on sanctity.

It we examine the character of Torquemada in the light of modern knowledge we find something which is far from saintly in his attitude towards the Jews whom he hated with a fanaticism beyond even that which he had for relapsed *Moriscos* and Protestants.

Why did Torquemada earn for himself the title of Scourge of the Jews? Why was he even more fanatically inhuman towards them than towards others who did not share his religious views?

Some historians believe that Tomás's grandfather, Alvar Fernandez de Torquemada, had introduced a 'Jewish taint' into the family when he married a Jewess. This was towards the end of the fourteenth century when the Jews were enjoying a respite from persecution. It was perfectly logical for this small nobleman, who may well have been financially embarrassed, to have brought money into the family by marrying the daughter of a rich Jew. He may have fallen in love with the Jewess. However, there is this suggestion that Alvar Fernandez brought Jewish blood into the family, and in Castile where, more than in other places, men and women were proud of their nobility and the purity of their blood, this was a deviation which would have its repercussions in the years to come.

A Castilian should be able to trace his ancestry back through the centuries; he should be able to boast of his *limpieza* – the purity of his blood.

Alvar Fernandez and his Jewish wife may have lived happily enough, but with the coming of Fernando Martinez and his wild preaching against the persecuted peoples, and with the mob risings and the rumours of Christian boys being crucified, it was not only an embarrassment to have Jewish blood in one's veins, it was also dangerous.

It will be remembered that Alonso de Spina, the Franciscan who had demanded that the Inquisition be established in Seville, was a *converso*, and that there were few more eager for the persecution of those Jews who, having been forced to accept baptism, had reverted to the practice of Judaism. There must have been an element of fear in de Spina's fanatical attack against his own people. Can the same judgment be applied to Tomás de Torquemada?

One imagines that knowledge ever present in his mind: in the blood of this fervent Catholic was that of the Jew. It may have been that in the days of his youth, before he was such an important man whom none would dare offend, he had been subjected to the sneers, the jeers, the humiliation which, for years, has been the burden of the Jewish race. It may have been that he sought to keep this a secret, that he lived in terror of its being discovered. Whatever the reason, if Torquemada really had this streak of Jewish blood in his veins, there can be no doubt that it does to some extent explain his fanatical hatred.

It is the writer, Hernando del Pulgar, Isabella's secretary, who tells of the Jewish blood in Torquemada; but his word is doubted by some historians who put forward the suggestion that Pulgar, himself a Jew and a New Christian, wished to bring into his own category a man who had proved himself the most zealous of all Catholics – and for this reason wrote as he did about Torquemada.

Geronimo Zurita writing later is insistent that Tomás de Torquemada was the possessor of 'clean blood', which meant that his veins had been uncontaminated, for it was believed that Jewish blood was dark, and pure Christian blood bright red!

It seems however that there is a good case for Pulgar's assertion, as the name of Tomás's grandmother is discreetly omitted by most Catholic writers.

When Sixtus IV, at the request of Isabella, called together a conference of Spanish Cardinals, certain rules were decided upon and briefs were sent to the Spanish Archbishops, instructing them to conduct the affairs of the Inquisition with integrity; and, should there be any Bishops of Jewish blood, these should not be allowed to deal personally with those affairs appertaining to the Inquisition, but should at all councils be represented by other prelates of high rank in their dioceses, always of course providing these men had no Jewish blood whatsoever in their veins.

Sabatini in *Torquemada and the Spanish Inquisition* states that this decree entirely contradicts Pulgar's assertion that Torquemada was of Jewish extraction. Yet it seems possible that a man as powerful as Torquemada would not have allowed himself to be pushed aside by such a decree; and as the Jewish grandmother is not mentioned by Catholic writers it may surely have been that, if Torquemada was eager to forget the Jewish strain, those about him were equally ready to help him.

As for Isabella herself, she was not averse to *conversos* as such; it was only when she heard stories of their reverting to their own faith that she was horrified. She kept many *conversos* in her own personal service. She would therefore have felt no revulsion towards Torquemada who was such a zealous Catholic, merely because he had a Jewish grandmother.

Moreover, although the Pope sent his instructions, Isabella and Ferdinand were determined that in Spain the Inquisition should be ordered by themselves with as little Papal interference as possible. Therefore I do not think that, because there was this clause in the Pope's instructions and because Torquemada was appointed by his sovereigns and accepted by the Pope as Grand Inquisitor of Castile and Aragon, this is a proof that he had no Jewish blood.

Such fanatical hatred as Torquemada's could be at the very root of his determination to destroy the Jews. His pride would have been deeply wounded by the knowledge that he was in part – however small – Jewish; and make no mistake about this: all the refusals of great offices, all the sleeping on planks, the privations and irritations pressed upon the human body, the hair shirt and the white wool of the Dominican robe under the black hood, the bare feet – all these were the outward signs of a man steeped in pride. But the simple people did not look within; they saw the ascetic face; they heard of the great renunciation of worldly goods, they saw the humble Dominican whose one desire was to serve the Faith. They did not see the cruel thirster after blood, the proud man who, terrified of what he considered the taint in himself, was determined to show the world how he would scourge those who were similarly tainted. The taint in Torquemada was nothing to do with the state of his blood; it was in the state of his proud and arrogant mind.

Yet had he lived in different times, had he been educated to tolerance, he might have been a good man. Intellectual he undoubtedly was, but how many intellects of the past – and the present – have been and are cursed with that blind spot, of which intolerance of other men's views is the outward sign?

Torquemada's great interest in life was in architecture, and it is said that, when he was with the simple workmen who carried out the projects in which he was interested, he cast off his fierce burning fanaticism and became a pleasant and kindly man. When money came to him, as it inevitably did, in his position of influence and importance, he used it, either for what he would call the glory of God, which was seeking those who did not agree with him and torturing and burning them at the stake, or for erecting great buildings such as the Church in Torquemada and the bridge over the River Pisuerga. The great achievement of his architectural ambitions was of course the Monastery of St Thomas at Avila, which took him ten years to complete; and after that it was his delight to use all the money, which he could spare from the expense of ferreting out heretics and apostates, in beautifying this magnificent monastery. It is significant that this beautiful building was used, not only as his residence, but also as the prison for his victims. Thereby it satisfied two ambitions. He had built one of the most magnificent monasteries in the country; and in its dungeons those accused of heresy were tortured.

There can be little doubt that when he was very young he yearned to lead a good life. It is interesting to speculate on the part chance played in his life. What if grandfather Alvar Fernandez had not married his Jewess? Would that fierce hatred never have existed? What if Tomás had never been called forth from his cloister to become the Queen's confessor? Would he have lived in quiet obscurity, pious, truly humble, happy in the quadrangles and cloisters of the Convent of Santa Cruz? Who can say?

When Torquemada was made Inquisitor-General he immediately began reforming the existing laws of the Inquisition and produced his 'Instructions' which consisted of twenty-eight articles.

In the first of these articles he explained the mode of procedure when the Inquisition was to be set in a place where hitherto it had not been. All the people must be summoned to the church, and the day chosen must be either a Sunday or a holiday. A sermon must be preached by the most eloquent preacher available or by one of the Inquisitors. When the sermon came to an end an announcement should be made that all faithful Christians must come forward to swear upon the Cross and the Gospels that they would favour the Inquisition and those who worked for it, and place no impediment in their way.

Then it should be announced that a period of grace was being allowed – it might be thirty or forty days – for all people who had committed heresy or apostasy, or who had practised Judaism, to come to the Inquisitors and confess. If they did this within the given time they would be charitably dealt with, providing their repentance was sincere and they told not only of their own sins but those of their neighbours.

There would, of course, be some punishment, for no one could offend against God's laws without punishment. (It seems strange that these men should have called themselves followers of the gentle Jesus and such haters of the Mosaic law, when thundering Jehovah would surely have been a God more suited to their needs and tastes.) But this penance should be light; that meant it would not be death at the stake, imprisonment, or confiscation of property and the impoverishment of the offender's family.

Those who confessed must write their confessions, and when they had performed their penances they must remember that although they were reconciled to the Church they had offended against the law of the land and that for this relapse they would not be allowed to wear ornaments of gold, silver, pearls or precious stones, nor dress in fine materials, nor ride on horseback, nor carry arms, for the whole of their lives. Morever they must not forget that they had sinned against Jesus Christ and, although, most mercifully, they were escaping their just due ('the fire') and they were being allowed to keep their property, they could be called upon to give up a portion of it. This would be used for a holy purpose – such as the war which Queen Isabella and King Ferdinand were pursuing against the Infidels of Granada, who as all knew, were enemies of the Holy Catholic Church. These penances would be decided on by the local Inquisitors, but they would depend on a guide which had been given them by the Reverend Father Prior of Holy Cross, Tomás de Torquemada.

Should a man or woman, who had fallen into heresy, fail to come forward during the period of grace, but offer his confession voluntarily afterwards, he would still be treated mercifully. That is, he would not be condemned to the fiery death. He would not be asked to give a portion of his estate because the *entire* estate would become forfeit to the Inquisition. He would suffer heavier penalties than those who had come forward earlier; and if the case were a bad one he might be awarded life imprisonment. But because he had come forward voluntarily he should not die by fire.

Children who had become heretics through the teaching of their parents should be treated leniently. If they were under twenty years of age and came forward voluntarily and informed the Inquisitors of the evil practices of their parents, they should be given very light penances and taught the true faith, for the merciful Inquisition excused them because they were young and had been led astray.

Any guilty of heresy and apostasy must lose all property, counting from the day of the first offence; so that, if a rich man knowing the Inquisition was about to arrest him decided to pass his property on to someone else, it could be confiscated by the Inquisition because it was the sinner's property at the time he committed heresy.

Heretics or Apostates who were arrested because of information given against them could ask for reconciliation to the Church, which might be allowed them provided they were sincere; this meant that they must inform against their friends. If it should be discovered that their confessions were not sincere, they would be immediately handed over to the secular arm for the death sentence.

If heresy or apostasy were not completely proved against a victim, the Inquisitors would be allowed to put the prisoner to torture. If, while being tortured, the heretic confessed his sins, he must repeat his confession during the next three days.

The publication of the names of witnesses was forbidden because, the instructions suggested, there had been cases of witnesses who, coming forward to the assistance of the Inquisition, had been wounded or killed by heretics. When the victim of the investigation had been proved guilty, an account of the evidence against him might be published as long as the names of the witnesses were withheld, together with any information which might lead to their identification. Suspects would be allowed to have their advocates who must however swear that, when they considered the prisoner guilty they would withdraw from the case. (It would have been a very brave advocate indeed who continued with the defence of a victim in the face of opposition from the Inquisition; he would need to be a man who was ready to brave examination, torture and the fire itself.)

If a suspected heretic, hearing of his impending capture, had managed to escape, an edict should be put on the church doors all through the district, ordering him to present himself to the Inquisitors within thirty days. If he did not do so his guilt was considered proved.

When heresy was proved against a dead man, there should be a trial and, if there was proof of guilt, his body should be dug up and committed to the flames, and his property should be confiscated. His family might defend him, but if they failed to prove him innocent they would suffer the penalties which fell to the children of condemned heretics.

The Inquisitors were to penetrate the small domains of petty overlords and there be treated as they were in lands belonging to the crown. Should such petty lords who ruled their lands decline to admit the Inquisition, then they should be considered guilty of aiding and abetting heresy.

Young people who were minors or unmarried and whose parents had been executed for heresy were to pass into the hands of the Inquisitors, that they might be instructed in the Faith and brought up as good Catholics. The royal bounty alms would provide for these, and girls should be given a small dowry that they might marry or go into convents. (Llorente states that in his persual of the archives of the Inquisition he sought in vain for a case of a child of a condemned parent who had been so cared for.)

Although the property of a man or woman, who had been guilty of heresy and had become reconciled to the Church, would be confiscated, any they should inherit *after* repentance they might keep.

Slaves of heretics might gain their freedom. (Was this an invitation to slaves to inform against their masters?) And even if a reconciled heretic were allowed to keep a part of his property he should not keep his slaves.

No officers connected with the Inquisition must receive gifts from the suspected. If they did so they might suffer excommunication; they would be required to forfeit twice the value of any gifts they had received. (Clearly a precaution against bribery.)

Any difference of opinion arising between Inquisitors must be submitted to Torquemada for his judgment.

Should any Inquisitor be found guilty of misdemeanour, he must be judged mercifully; and if he persisted in his ill conduct, then should Torquemada be informed and the offender should be replaced.

If any matter arose which was not provided for by the articles of the Instruction, the Inquisitors should themselves decide what must be done in the service of their Royal Highnesses and for the glory of God and the Faith.

This is the gist of the twenty-eight articles set out by Torquemada, which were to be made use of by Inquisitors in the centuries to come.

Austere, self-righteous, determined to mould men in his own image, ever eager to deal out fearful punishment to those who had failed to embrace the privations which he forced on himself, Torquemada would have desired to see the methods employed by the Inquisitors used for other purposes besides the condemnation of heretics and apostates.

In the case of bigamy he declared that this should be a matter for the Inquisitors, for marriage was a sacrament and any who defiled it had offended against the laws of God. Sodomy should also be dealt with by the Inquisition, and those who were found guilty should suffer death by burning.

Thus new fears were growing within that land over which Torquemada held great power.

It was only natural that, while Torquemada dealt out terrible punishments for those who had been guilty of immorality, there should be whispers of the conduct of certain priests; and these murmurs caused a great deal of sorrow to Torquemada.

He knew that it was true that the reputation of the clergy was not as pure as it should be. Torquemada would have liked to sweep through the Church in the guise of an avenging angel and, discovering those who had sullied the name of Holy Church, deal with them as he dealt with heretics.

There was one offence which was looked upon with particular distaste. This was a habit – not infrequent – of priests, who lured attractive young women to the confessional where they did all in their power to seduce them. At this time priest and penitent were together during the confession, not separated as they were after the sixteenth century – a custom which was very probably introduced because of the licentious habits of the priests.

It was somewhat difficult for Torquemada to expose this habit, for to do so would bring great shame on the Church; and another reason was that instructions for the clergy must come from Rome, and the Pope at this time, Innocent VIII, was a man who had presumably made no great effort to subdue the lusts of the flesh. He was a family man, with his children about him in the Vatican; he delighted in them and showered great honours upon them. So, if the Pope himself indulged in amorous conduct, it would be rather cynical and hypocritical for him to condemn some poor priest for a little waywardness while listening to an account of the sins of some attractive penitent.

However so rampant was this crime of the confessional – *solicitatio ad turpia* – that something had to be done about it, and the conduct of several priests was examined, found to be at fault, and sentences passed.

These however were very slight – necessarily so if the Church was not going to be brought into ill repute.

John Marchant cites one case in which Joseph Peralta, Friar of the Order of St Jerome, committed sodomy with John Romeo, a young boy of fourteen who was in his care. This crime being discovered, it was necessary to pass judgment. The Friar was therefore sentenced to a year's confinement in his monastery, but was allowed to celebrate Mass. The young boy, however, not being a priest, must be treated more severely. He was led through the streets and, at the corner of each, five lashes were administered. On the child's head was placed a mitre covered in feathers, which was to all who watched an indication of the nature of his crime. The boy, we are told, died after the whipping; the priest – presumably because he *was* a priest – resumed his merry life, ready, no doubt, after a sentence which was by no means a real punishment, to seduce any suitable young boy who came under his care.

Marchant also quotes the case of Father Pueyo, who was made Father Confessor to the Nuns of Our Mother St Monica. Pueyo promptly seduced five of the nuns, and when this was discovered, even though he was a priest, it was agreed that this was a sin which could not be lightly passed over. When he was brought before the Inquisitors and asked to explain his sinful conduct, he replied that he had been sent to the Nuns that he might take care of them. He had done so as a faithful servant and said to the Inquisitors: '*Domine quinque talenta tradidisti mihi me, ecce alia quinque super lucratus sum.*' To which the Inquisitors, highly amused, replied: '*Peccata tua remittuntur tibi, nunc vade in pace, et noli amplius peccare.*'

His response, which had so amused the Inquisitors, had brought him freedom even from the light penance which he would otherwise have been expected to do.

It seems that the only punishment bestowed on the priests who had misconducted themselves was an order to abstain from hearing confessions and a short confinement in a monastery.

There is no doubt though that Torquemada abhorred the loose behaviour of the priests and probably realized the need to repress it, but had he been as stern with the priests as he was with those he suspected of heresy, Martin Luther would not have had such a good case to lay before his audiences in the century to come. But, of course, Torquemada's real venom was reserved for heretics and the Jews whom he hated with such a fierce passion.

He had already given Isabella and Ferdinand good proof of his hatred of the Moors. When Ferdinand has been making an assault on Granada, and had been in difficulties (his men were smitten with fever and he had no money with which to carry on the campaign), news of the King's troubles reached Torquemada, who at that time was deeply engrossed in the building of St Thomas's monastery at Avila. Torquemada thereupon called his mule-driver to him and filled the water-jugs, which were on the backs of the twelve mules, with gold which he had intended to spend on the building of the monastery. These he sent in the charge of the muleteer, to Isabella, with a message explaining that the money was for the continuance of the war against the Moors.

It was true that this money proved useless, for Ferdinand's armies were too sick to fight, whatever weapons were put at their disposal, and Ferdinand was obliged to raise the siege of Loja. But this gesture was an indication to the Catholic sovereigns of what an ardent supporter they had in the austere Dominican.

Here was a man, they believed, whom they could trust. Doubtless this incident was one of many which influenced them when the question of setting up the Supreme Council arose, and again when the time came to elect the Inquisitor-General of Castile and Aragon.

CHAPTER EIGHT

THE HOLY HOUSE AND TORTURE

When a man or woman was suspected of heresy, he or she was brought to a special chamber, reserved for this purpose, in the building which was used as the headquarters of the Inquisition. This building would be called the Casa Santa, the Holy House or the Holy Office.

The word of two witnesses, provided the evidence they gave was not substantially divergent, was enough to condemn, but instructions had been laid down, by Torquemada and those who had come before him, as to the treatment of *suspected* heretics.

The method of treating these unfortunate people was grossly unjust and exactly what would be expected, for the great desire of the Inquisitors was to bring as many victims as possible into their clutches; and the great desire of the sovereigns was to establish a country which was entirely Catholic, and at the same time receive confiscated goods into the state exchequer. Therefore men and women who were proved to be innocent were of little use.

Each victim, when he received the dread summons, must have known that he had very little chance of going free. His main hope would surely have been to escape torture and painful death. When faced with these horrors, perhaps the loss of his worldly goods and a life of imprisonment seemed bearable.

It often happened that victims were arrested at night. There would be the sudden knock on the door, and when this was opened, the *alguazils* or familiars of the Inquisition would demand entrance; and if there was any resistance force their way in.

The victim would then be told to dress and prepare to leave immediately. Some European countries in the twentieth century imitated the methods of the Inquisitors, and there can surely be no method more calculated to arouse terror in peaceful citizens. The sudden knock in the night, for which, after this inhuman method had become a custom, all men and women must have listened, would have been as alarming as an air-raid warning of the 1939–1945 War – only more so, because with the latter there was merely the possibility of pain and death, whereas with the former there was the certainty of the first, even if it should prove possible to escape the second.

The *alguazils* were very eager that the arrest should be made silently. Perhaps it was all part of the mental torture they had contrived. A man would be seen by his family, friends, and neighbours one day; the next he would have disappeared into the grim prisons of the Inquisition, perhaps only to emerge in the ghastly procession to the *auto de fé,* or at best to return robbed of his possessions, his body doubtless mangled and mutilated by their hideous torture machines.

The swift and silent removal was certainly sinister; should the victim cry out and threaten to wake the neighbourhood, he was gagged. There was an instrument which when it was shut was shaped like a pear. It could be enlarged by means of screws, and was forced into the mouth, then extended so that the victim was obliged to keep his mouth open, being quite unable to move his jaws. It was, as can be imagined, very painful and effective.

Once inside the Casa Santa, the prisoner would be 'tried'. Every effort was made to strike him with terror so that he was in a state of such nervousness as would make him ready to admit all the charges which were brought against him.

The room into which he was taken was hung with black, presumably to remind him that he was already in the presence of death – and, poor man, it might have been happier for him if he had come immediately to that state. No light came through the windows; but on a table, which was set at one end of the room and covered with black velvet, there was an image of Christ on the cross, and six lighted candles. There was also a copy of the Bible on this table. Beside the table was a pulpit on which stood another candle; and at this pulpit sat a secretary who would read out the crimes of which the victim was accused.

The Inquisitors would be seated at the table in their white habits and black hoods; and the guards who had brought the prisoner from his house would be ranged behind him when he had been brought to stand before the table.

The Inquisitor-in-chief would take no notice whatever of the prisoner for some minutes, during which time he would pretend to be absorbed in the papers which lay before him. This was according to the 'instructions' and was calculated to increase the prisoner's fear, which it assuredly did, for he must wonder what those papers contained to make the Inquisitor interested in them to such an extent that he appeared to be quite oblivious of the poor creature who was waiting, in a state of terror, for his attention.

Eventually the Inquisitor would put aside the papers, and the secretary would ask the prisoner for his name, address and other particulars.

Then the cold eyes of the Inquisitor would be turned upon him. Did he know why he had been arrested? he would be asked.

The poor bewildered man – who, it was very likely, had not the faintest notion why he had been arrested – would declare his innocence, at which the Inquisitor – again acting on 'instructions' – would turn to the papers on the table and appear to study them significantly.

Had the man any enemies? Did he attend confession regularly?

His victim would know that he must answer truthfully, for the Inquisitor would then quickly fire a series of questions. What was his diocese? Who was his confessor? When did he last go to confession?

The Inquisitors were warned not to be moved by the terror of the prisoner. Should the man break down and weep, tell heartrending stories about his family, assure the Inquisitors that he was a good Catholic, they must not allow themselves to be moved. Heretics, they were reminded, were crafty. Had they not pretended to follow the Catholic Faith and practised heresy in secret? Again and again Inquisitors were reminded that the condemnation of one might be the salvation of thousands, for there were plausible heretics who not only sinned against the

Church themselves, but inveigled others into doing likewise.

The aim of these interviews was to make the victim break down and confess and, in confessing, incriminate as many of his family and neighbours as possible.

If however the prisoner was a stubborn man, a bold man, who refused to be intimidated by the guards, the Inquisitor and the gloomy solemnity of the chamber, then other tactics must be used.

Then the Inquisitor should allow his expression to soften, he should speak to the prisoners as though for their own good, tell them that he wished them no harm, that he felt towards them as a father who sees his child straying into evil ways. What would a father's feelings be in such circumstances? Regret! Eagerness to lead the straying child back to holy paths! That was how the Inquisitors felt. A confession could do so much. It could ease the soul of its burden of sin, it could bring pardon, sudden release. What should the Inquisition say to one who was truly penitent but: 'Come back to the Church. You are forgiven'?

True penitents naturally abhorred heresy, and in their commission of this great sin they could not have been alone. There must be others who were secretly sinful. Those who were regretful of past sins would wish to give others a chance of penitence. Therefore, when they gave to the Inquisitors the names of those who had shared their sin, then and only then could there be no doubt of their true penitence.

This method was very successful. Many fell into the trap laid for them; and thus more and more victims were brought into the prisons of the Inquisition.

If however a man persisted in his innocence, insisting that he knew none who was heretic, he would be taken away to a cell and brought back again. There would be hours of questions, threats and cajoling, and if at the end of them he remained obdurate, the Inquisitor would shrug his shoulders and tell him that he had been called away and could question him no more for some little time. As he had not proved his innocence he would remain a prisoner until the Inquisitor's return.

If the prisoner continued to remain firm, more cunning methods would be tried. He would be told that he appeared to be innocent after all but, because his jailors were not entirely convinced, they must still keep him a prisoner. He would be removed to a more comfortable cell, and certain selected visitors would be allowed to see him. Thus his confidence would return and those who visited him would be instructed to encourage him to be careless in his talk. A stray word on which a certain meaning could be placed, and the Inquisitors might have what they sought. These visitors would invariably implore the prisoner to make his confession, assuring him that if he did so he would be discharged with a light penance.

What the prisoner did not know was that one of the officers of the Inquisition, in a place of concealment, was taking down all that was said during the interview.

Sometimes even this plan did not work, for the prisoner might be entirely innocent of heresy. Then a little trick was employed. The prisoner would share his cell with another who the prisoner would think was in the same position as himself but who was in actuality an agent of the Inquisition. The task of this man would be to talk to the prisoner during the long hours they were alone, to discuss his own pretended heresy, talk of his beliefs and trap the prisoner into damning admissions.

If however all these methods failed, the prisoner was brought once more into the chamber to stand before the table on which stood the cross, the candle and the gospels. Questions were fired at him at great speed; and this went on for a very long time, until at last the weary prisoner was bewildered into contradicting himself.

He was lying he would be told. Then he would be taken away. His next journey would be to the torture chamber.

It was during the rule of Torquemada that torture became such an important part of the work of the Inquisition. Earlier there had been reluctance to employ it; and there is mention, in a letter written by Philip IV of France (1268–1314), of the torturing of heretics, which method had been newly introduced by the Inquisition. Philip did protest against the harshness of the torture, although certainly he had no objection to its being used when he so desired it, as in the case of the Templars.

Clement V arranged that there should be an enquiry into the

methods used by the Inquisitors, when he received protests that men and women were so severely tortured that they confessed to heresy knowing that if they did not they would die under torture.

These were the beginnings, and between this time (early fourteenth century) and the establishment of the Inquisition in Castile (in the late fifteenth century) there are not a great many records of torture; although of course it is very possible that many cases were not recorded.

According to Article 15 in Torquemada's instructions, the Inquisitors were given permission to torture where heresy is 'halfproven'. They were warned however that there must be no shedding of blood, because it was against the laws of the Church for a priest to shed the blood of another human being. It might seem that a little true Christianity was finding its way into the Inquisition, but this was not so. There was a hasty proviso: If, under torture, a victim died, the Inquisitor responsible must seek immediate absolution through his fellow priest. Each priest had the absolute right bestowed by Torquemada to absolve the murderer of his sin.

Thus it appears that whenever there is a hint of leniency or justice shining through these cruel laws, there always follows the quick adjustment, the sleight-of-hand as it were, to turn justice into mockery and kindness into fiendish cruelty.

There were several stages of torture. This was characteristically referred to by the pious Inquisitors, not as torture which was a harsh word, but as The Question.

The uses of torture had been laid down by Nicolaus Eymeric, who had been Grand Inquisitor of Aragon in the fourteenth century; and he had been inspired in the work he compiled by that of Bernard Gui written in the early part of that century.

Torquemada must have agreed with a great deal that these two had written, for he allowed much of it to stand and form a basis for his Instructions.

Eymeric had advised Inquisitors that there should be five stages of torture and each was important, for even during the early stages a confession might be wrung from the victim.

The first of the five stages was the Threat. This was delivered to the prisoner who, having heard a great deal about this terrible weapon of the cruel men into whose hands he had fallen, might become weak with horror when he was told that he was in danger of experiencing it.

The second was the journey to the torture chamber. Slowly, ceremonially, he would be led to that dismal room, lighted by candles and the glow of braziers which held their own hideous and significant meaning; he would be given time to glance round the room of pain, at the instruments ready for use, perhaps at one or two of the victims who were already receiving the attention of the black-robed fiends (their appearance was calculated to inspire terror; they wore black cowls over their heads and in these small holes had been cut that they might peer through them at their victims), perhaps hear groans of misery and screams of agony. A very important one, this second stage.

The third was even more terrifying (for these stages by their very nature grew more alarming as they followed one another). The prisoner was seized and stripped of his clothes, in readiness for the torture.

And the fourth – that was showing him the instrument which was to be used, strapping his naked body upon it and giving him time to savour the terrible knowledge that his time of agony was at hand.

If he had passed this fourth stage without confessing and giving the names of other sinners, then he was indeed a bold man; and there was nothing to delay passing on to the fifth and last stage. The pulley was hoisted; the rack turned. The physical torture had begun.

By law it was forbidden to *repeat* torture, so that a sufferer, having once endured the Question and maintained his or her innocence, must not be put to the test again. The Inquisitors found this an easy hurdle. Instead of *repeating* the torture, they *continued* it day after day, and any interval was a mere *suspension*.

The three tortures used more frequently than others in the dungeons of the Inquisition were the rack, the hoist and the water torture.

The method of the rack is well known, for it was in universal use.

The hoist was perhaps more commonly used in the dungeons of the Inquisition than any other torture, no doubt because it was the easiest to inflict, yet as painful as others.

The sufferer on the hoist had his arms tied behind his back, and the rope which bound them was passed over a pulley fixed to the ceiling. The victim was slowly drawn upwards so that his arms had to support the whole weight of his body. The pain was excruciating, and the victim would be lowered after a few minutes and told to confess. If he failed to do this he was pulled upwards once more, and so violently that his joints might be dislocated. Thus did he suffer a new and more exquisite torture. Again he was invited to confess and, if once more he failed to do so, weights were tied to his feet and the jerks began again. If after this he persisted in his refusal to confess to heresy and implicate others, he was left hanging in such pain as it is not easy to imagine.

When he became unconscious he was taken down, but the torture was not ended; it was merely suspended. The Inquisitors must remember the law (no man or woman must be tortured twice); it had merely been necessary to call a halt in the proceedings which would be continued as soon as the victim was able to feel pain once more.

The water torture was very popular with the Inquisitors, no doubt because it was particularly cruel. In this the victim was tied to a ladder, which was placed in a slightly sloping position, the feet higher than the head. Wrists and ankles were very tightly tied so that the rope cut into the flesh when the victim moved them. The head was held firmly in position by a band of metal, and the mouth opened forcibly by a piece of iron; pieces of wood were thrust into the nostrils, and over the mouth was placed a long piece of linen. When the victim was thus secured, jars of water were brought forward and slowly poured down his throat. The water carried the linen with it. The poor creature would automatically swallow and by so doing take the linen down his gullet; and as he struggled the cord would cut into his body where it bound him. Not until he was half dead from asphyxia would the linen be hauled back and the treatment be 'suspended', to be 'continued later'.

Although the rack, the hoist and the water torture were the

main methods used by the Inquisitors, there were others equally diabolical.

One of these was the Spanish Chair. This consisted of an iron chair with rests for the arms. The sufferer must sit in this chair with an iron band about his neck and arms to keep them in one position. His bare feet were placed in stocks very close to a brazier. Then the feet were coated with fat and slowly allowed to roast; and so that the flesh might not burn too quickly, fat was continually applied.

Flogging was practised, as was the cutting off of toes and fingers by a gradual process, perhaps one each day. People were hung in the torture chamber, suspended by their thumbs, with weights attached to their feet.

Limborch, in his *History of the Inquisition*, tell a piteous story of a Jew (a new Christian) who was brought before the Inquisition having been betrayed by a servant whom he had whipped for theft.

He was arrested and, when he refused to admit that he was a heretic, was told that he would be taken to the torture chamber. This was the first stage of the Torture: The Threat. He insisted that he spoke truthfully and the Inquisitors answered that, since he was so obstinate, he clearly chose to suffer torture, and in this case the Inquisition could not be held guilty if his blood was shed or he died while it was being applied. The Inquisitors were as dexterous with words and as expert at handling their own consciences as they were with the terrible machines they used.

The first of the tortures in this case was to put him in a linen bag and tie this so tightly about him that he was almost suffocated, but not quite. Then the bag was untied and he was freed, and once more asked to confess. Refusing to do so, his thumbs were bound with cords so tightly that the blood spurted up from under the nails. Still he refused. He was then made to stand with his back to the wall on which were several pulleys fitted with ropes. These ropes were fastened about his legs, arms and other parts of his tormented body; then the ropes were violently jerked so that his joints were dislocated; and finally, still not confessing, he was left suspended by the ropes.

Remaining, as these men would say, 'obstinate', he was

struck with a ladder-like instrument on the shins with such force that he fainted with the pain. He was then bound with ropes which were pulled so tight that they cut into the flesh, making wounds; tighter and tighter were the ropes drawn; and the torture only stopped because much of the man's blood was shed and he was close to death. The Inquisitiors, knowing that should a victim die whilst in their hands they would be exonerated, yet did not wish to let too many victims die. Their intention was to preserve them that they might be handed over to the secular arm which would then pronounce sentence of death; for it was convenient that these holy men should not be said to have caused the death of anyone.

This particular Jew was eventually released, made to wear the garment of shame – the *Sanbenito* – for two years, and then banished from Seville. Surely, but for their love of inflicting pain, the sentence of banishment would have been given in the first place.

Accounts of torture suffered by men and women who fell into the hands of Inquisitors is so harrowing to write and to read that one is tempted to slur over details, and to make the account of them as brief as possible, to leave to the imagination the terrible suffering which was inflicted on unfortunate people who were not being punished for doing harm to anyone, but merely for using their brains. But there again, in using the word punishment, I may be told by some supporters of this evil institution, that I am wrong. Torture was not inflicted as a punishment. Heretics were tortured that they might confess their sins, that they might betray their friends, and that thus these holy men who set themselves up in their arrogance to teach the world, might lead them to salvation.

Yet, if we are going to examine the Inquisition, how is it possible to overlook this shocking cruelty which was at its very roots?

In *The History of the Inquisition as it Subsists in the Kingdoms of Spain and Portugal to this Day*, compiled and translated by the Reverend J. Barker, M.A. in 1734, there are some horrifying accounts of cruelties inflicted by the Inquisition. One account tells of William Lithgow, a Scotsman, who was arrested in Malaga, accused of being a spy. Since he was a

Protestant he was immediately pressed to become a Catholic. Refusing to change his religion he was loaded with irons, and his legs were extended by means of an iron bar, a yard long, of such weight that he was unable either to stand or to sit and could only lie flat on his back. He was given only a pint of water every other day, and had no bed, pillow or blanket; the window in his room was closed up with lime and stone and the orders were that he was to have nothing that 'bears any likeness to comfort'.

Forty-seven days after his imprisonment he heard a coach draw up outside his prison; officials of the Inquisition entered and took him away to a place where he was to be tortured. Unable to walk, he had to be carried; and when the irons were knocked off, so clumsy were his tormentors that they took away an inch of his heel with the iron. He was racked for five hours and taken back to his prison. It was arranged that every morning at a certain hour a coach should drive up and stop close to his window so that he might suffer the additional torment of believing that once more he was to be taken away to be tortured.

He was left in his noisome prison where he became 'overrun with vermin which crawled in clusters about his beard, lips and eyebrows so that he could scarce open his eyes' With a great show of magnanimity it was ordered that he was to be swept free of vermin twice every eight days.

Furious because they could not shake this man's belief in his version of the gospels, he was kicked in the face by an Inquisitor and sentenced to undergo eleven different tortures. These he survived and was then condemned to be carried to Granada to be burned alive.

A Turkish slave and a Negress, also a slave, who had been charged to look after him that he might be preserved for the fire, showed him great kindness; and another servant, a Flemish boy, was so struck with the amazing courage of this man that he carried the story of his sufferings to some Englishmen who were in the town; because of this the case was taken before Sir Walter Afton, the English Ambassador. Thus Mr Lithgow's return to England was made possible. He was carried on a feather bed to the King, James I, to whom he told his story, and we have yet another account of the inhumanity of the Inquisition, not only towards the Spanish, but towards foreigners who ventured into their country.

Another account (this comes from the same J. Baker and John Marchant) is of an event which took place in the eighteenth century when the French, reaching Aragon, are said to have rescued several young girls who had been taken up by the Inquisitors. These girls, we are told, were taken from their homes during the night – not because of their religious beliefs, but because of their physical attractions. They were shown various instruments of torture and told that, unless they complied with the desires of their captors, these instruments would be used upon them.

One girl is reputed to have stated that she was shown a large brass pan with a cover which was placed on an oven. In the oven a fire burned. She was told that heretics were put in the pan and the cover placed over them, when a slow fire was kept going in the oven until the contents of the pan were reduced to ashes. The girl also tells of a wheel, from the inside circumference of which protruded sharp knives. Those who spoke against the Pope and priests were put on the wheel which was turned until they were cut to pieces. A pit full of snakes was also shown to her; this was for people who did not pay proper respect to holy images. The girl was told that unless she submitted to the will of the Inquisitor it would be the pan over the oven for her.

This is the wildest story of all, but there is no doubt that the Inquisitors had power over the life and death of a great many people, and such power inevitably corrupts. There were lascivious priests – there always have been – and the laws of celibacy which were imposed doubtless increased that lasciviousness; and while Popes openly flaunted their families in the Vatican itself, how could continence be expected of priests?

One of the instruments of torture, which was discovered in the prison of the Inquisition in Toledo by the Invading French, was a statue built to resemble the Virgin Mary. The front of this statue was covered with sharp nails and knives.

Levers were pulled, and the arms of the statue would embrace its victim who would be crushed tighter and tighter, while the knives and nails pierced the naked flesh. How ironic, and yet how apt, to have made this statue in the form of the Virgin Mary! What a commentary on the mockery these men had made of the Christian Faith!

The case of a certain Elvira del Campo, who was the wife of a scrivener, is quoted at length by Henry Charles Lea (*A History of the Spanish Inquisition* Vol III), who takes it from the records of the Toledo Inquisition; it is again quoted by Cecil Roth in his book *The Spanish Inquisition*; but it is so shocking and at the same time so revealing that I feel it should be briefly cited here.

Elvira was arrested because she had put on clean linen on a Saturday and refused to eat pork. This happened in the middle of the sixteenth century, almost a hundred years after Torquemada had established the Inquisition in Spain.

She had no intention to commit heresy she declared; but her tormentors showed her the dreaded instruments in their foul chamber, and the poor woman, falling to her knees in terror, begged them to tell her what they wished her to do; she declared she would do anything rather than suffer the torment.

She was told to tell the truth, and demanded piteously what they wished her to say, for she had told the truth. Cords were tied to her arms and twisted; and between her screams of pain she cried out: 'Señors, tell me what I have to say. I do not know what I have done. Loosen me, and I will tell the truth. I do not know what you wish me to say but only tell me, and I will say it.' Again and again the cords were tightened; again she was commended to tell the truth and she continued to assure them that, if only they would tell her what to say, she would say it.

She was clearly a women of little education, and it seems to have been sheer brutality in this case which goaded those fiends to continue.

She had not eaten pork, she said, because pork made her sick; she did not like pork. 'I have done nothing,' she continued. 'Release me and I will tell you the truth. I don't know what I have to tell but loosen me ... tell me what I have to tell, and I will tell it. Say. Say.'

And still they continued to torture her.

What had she done which was contrary to the Holy Catholic Church? they demanded.

'Release me,' she moaned. 'Take me from here. Only tell me what I have to say. Oh ... wretched me! I will tell you all that is wanted. Señors, you are breaking my arms. Loosen me ...'

She must tell in detail what she really had done.

'What am I wanted to tell? I did everything. Oh, loosen me, for I don't remember what I have to tell. I am a weak woman and my arms are breaking. Have you no pity for a weak woman?'

They told her they would have pity for her if she would tell the truth. 'Señors,' she cried then, 'tell me, tell me it ...' Again the torture was applied. 'I don't know how to tell it, Señor,' she wailed. 'I don't know.'

The account goes on with the continual repetition which is so heartrending. Again and again she professes her willingness to say whatever they want her to say, but she does not know what it is. She has not eaten pork. Pork makes her sick, and she does not like pork. She has changed her linen on a Saturday. But then her linen needed to be changed. She had meant no harm; and she does not know what they want of her.

It was impossible for her to satisfy them, for they were taking what they wanted; they wished to torture her; they placed her naked body on the frame and she was given the water torture (not the torture of the same name which has already been described, but the more modern form, during which the body was painfully stretched, a funnel placed in the throat and jars of water poured into the mouth).

The account is punctuated by the agonized pleas of this woman. Always it is: '*Remind* me what I have to say, for I do not know. I do not know how to tell it. I pray you tell me how to tell it. I say I did it – whatever you wish me to have done – but, my God, how can I tell it?'

Eventually they 'suspended' the torture, but they renewed

it after a lapse of four days. Again she begged to be told what to say and it may have been that her tormentors conveyed this to the poor dazed mind, for she admitted that she had practised Judaism, declared she was penitent and begged for reconciliation to the Holy Catholic Church. This was granted at an *auto de fé*. And although many suffered even greater torment than Elvira del Campo, the detailed description of what took place in the torture chamber when all her remarks were recorded gives one of the clearest – and for that very reason most horrible – pictures of the Inquisition at work.

One of the most nauseating tortures of all was that in which a large dish was turned upside-down on the naked stomach of the victim. In the dish were placed several mice, and a fire was lighted on top of the dish. This caused panic among the mice, and as the dish grew hotter they burrowed into the flesh of the sufferer. This was similar to that of the ant torture which is said to be carried out by some natives in Africa.

The most terrible of tortures, such as that just described and burying alive, were used by the Inquisitors in the Netherlands when the savage attempt was made to turn that Protestant nation into a Catholic one.

Many of the stories which have been recorded cannot be accepted as truth in their entirety; but even allowing the exaggerations there can be no doubt that one of the most unhappy fates which could have befallen a man during any age was to have been taken – a suspected heretic – into the building which was known as Casa Santa, the Holy House.

CHAPTER NINE

THE SECULAR ARM AND THE
AUTO DE FÉ

If one did not burn with indignation at the plight of tens of thousands, one could laugh at the method of passing sentence on them.

The holy men of the Church, who had been torturing the bodies of those unfortunate men and women were unable to deliver the death sentence, for a Christian must not shed the blood of a fellow creature! So the Inquisitors, determined as they were that the mutilated bodies of their victims should be consigned to the flames, made sure of their salvation by allowing someone else to condemn them to it. They could piously wash their hands of the whole affair, turn their eyes to heaven and murmur: 'We have done our duty; we have tried all means within our power to bring these men and women back to Holy Church. We have failed, so there is nothing we can do but abandon them to the secular arm.'

They *abandoned* them; they did not *send* them. These men had to be very careful of their choice of words. It was the same deceitfulness as *suspending* not *repeating* the torture. Their image of their God, it seems, was of a potentate more powerful than themselves, equally vindictive, arrogant and vain, but slightly less intelligent since He could be so easily hoodwinked. The hasty absolution of a priest could exonerate a fellow practitioner if he had committed murder in the torture chamber – and God, it appeared, would be deceived by a hastily murmured penance. Thus they who had persecuted their victims, tricked them, tortured them, and determined on their death, were not guilty of murder because they merely murmured: 'The Church can help you no more. The Church casts you out and you are abandoned to the secular arm. This we do beseeching it at the same time to deal moderately with you without shedding your blood and putting you to death.'

They had one eye on Heaven as they uttered those words; they were for the ears of the recording angel. But woe betide any member of the secular arm who showed that mercy which they 'beseeched'. He should know better – and very quickly all secular officers did learn the rule; the plea for mercy was for their *sleeping* God's ear. It meant 'It was not we who did this murder. We are Christian priests. Our hands are clean. It is the secular arm which has felt it its duty to sentence to death these enemies of the state.'

As for the officers of the secular arm, what were they to do? Act leniently towards those who were abandoned by the Inquisition? And be themselves brought before the tribunal to answer a charge of heresy!

But even the Inquisitors had to admit that it was possible for a true Catholic to be accused of heresy, to be submitted to the torture and perhaps be unjustly condemned to death. They consoled themselves. What a glorious death! To die for the Faith and in the Faith. They would go straight to paradise. Of what had they to complain?

Many prisoners who had been urged to repent and promised mercy if they did so, learned that they had not escaped the death penalty. The only mercy they would be shown was strangulation before their bodies were burned – which they had to agree would be a far less painful death than that of being burned alive. They were told that it was God who would have mercy on them; the secular arm must punish them in accordance with the law, and the punishment for heretics was death. This had been so since the Bull of Innocent IV, issued as far back as the fourteenth century, which compelled the officers of the secular arm to execute heretics or themselves suffer excommunication and trial for heresy.

Sentence on heretics – relapsed or reconciled – was to take place in public so that the scene might be witnessed by a large number of people. The ceremony, religious, barbaric, and a ritual massacre, was called an Act of Faith – *auto de fé* in Spanish but perhaps more commonly known as the Portuguese *auto da fé*. Sunday was considered quite the best day for this hideous spectacle to take place, because Sunday was a holy day; moreover more people were free to see the sights. It was good for the people to see what happened to those who sinned against the laws of Holy Church; it filled them with fear and determination that they would not stand among those wretched men and women. It was looked upon as a rehearsal for Judgment Day.

The Inquisitor was a person of great power. He was given the right to grant Indulgences, and there can be no doubt that many used this power to extract the information they desired. What a weapon to place in the hands of these men whose mission in life was to bring heretics to, what they would call, justice! How simple to say to those who felt the burden of their sins heavy upon them: 'Come, tell me what you know of these men and women. Give me a good case against them, and in exchange you shall receive the indulgence you crave.' Naturally the superstitious were ready to comply, and if they had no real information, how could they resist fabricating it, and perhaps so deluding themselves as to believe it was the truth?

Inquisitors, in their privileged position, could be excommunicated only by the Pope himself; and the Popes, who regarded the Inquisitors as their servants, in spite of the continual struggle with the various monarchs who were constantly on the alert to free their countries from Papal influence, naturally gave them their protection.

This protection was extended to all those who served, even in a less significant degree, under the Inquisitors. Each Inquisitor had many helpers. There were vicars, *socii*, familiars, notaries, and many others who performed the less important tasks necessary to deal with heretics, from the arrest to the *auto de fé*.

The vicars, or delegates as they were sometimes called, were really the understudies of the Inquisitor. When he was not available, or engaged with some very important victim, these vicars would take over his duties; and a great deal of the preliminaries which were simply routine were conducted by them. They were, in effect, Inquisitors in embryo.

The *socii* who accompanied the Inquisitor on his journeys, had no special official duty, but having followed the case as closely as had the Inquisitor himself, their function was to discuss the case with the Inquisitor and occasionally offer an opinion.

The familiars formed the Inquisitor's guard – a very personal guard. They were not necessarily priests, but usually came from more worldly callings, although, once having become a familiar, a man automatically became part of a half-religious order. Some of these familiars carried arms, for Inquisitors were naturally not beloved by the people, and must constantly be on the alert for attack from those who sought revenge on behalf of some loved one. Familiars were frequently in the prisons of the Inquisition; they visited prisoners and urged them to repent. It was generally a familiar who was used to visit a prisoner in the guise of a kindly friend, offering advice, luring the prisoner to make some careless remark which could be used against him. There was no need for them to be of high social standing; and it was of no importance what work they had done before joining the community. It was for this reason that they made such good spies. They could appear to be ordinary men of the work-a-day world so much more easily then could those who had spent years in seclusion. Of all the community concerned with the torturing and burning of mankind, next to the Inquisitors themselves, the familiars seem the most sinister.

The notary's was a position not easy to fill, for there were few humble enough to want it, who were sufficiently educated. The duties of the notary were to keep records of the examinations and questions and answers, given under torture; moreover records had to be kept so that those reconciled heretics who relapsed later should not be able to escape the stake. The records had to be written in Latin, which seems to have given the notaries unnecessary trouble, for the questions and answers were naturally spoken in the language of the people concerned. We owe a great deal to these notaries and their records; but for them, Llorente would never have had an opportunity of going through the archives and discovering so much of what happened.

Other servants of the Inquisition were bishops, abbés and sometimes lawyers. But the bishops and the Inquisitors from the earliest days had been on uneasy terms. The bishop had at one time been the arbiter of religious conduct and never did he happily accept the power of the Inquisitor.

The Inquisition was devoted to formality; it was very eager to show the world that a great deal of thought had gone into the compilation of its laws. Again there is a hint of that hypocrisy which overshadows everything that was done. The Inquisition, on the surface, was a well-organized institution, the laws of which had been studied and adjusted during the centuries and in the light of experience. It was very important that it should appear to be an efficient organization, far above petty malice or love of cruelty for its own sake. The brutality must appear to be for the good of all concerned – only thus could men, even such as these, convince themselves that they were not inhuman monsters. It is all in line with their talk of 'suspended' not 'repeated' torture, and keeping the stain of murder from their souls by 'abandoning' their victims to the secular arm.

They had decided that there were several grades of heresy. *Affirmative* heretics were those who announced quite openly their divergence from the rigid line laid down by the Church, or their belief in another religion. *Negative* heretics were those who denied their heresy and, if they were forced to admit it, declared they had committed it in innocence. There were also *suspected* heretics who had shown evidence of conduct which might lead them to heresy, such as indulging in conversation with heretics or expressing pity for those who had been robbed of their goods or burned at the stake. Any man or woman suspected of heresy must make a formal announcement that he or she had no heretical tendency, and would in future remain outside the sphere of heretical influence.

Those who put obstacles in the path of the Inquisitors were also guilty of offence. There were – and this revives one's belief in human nature – many who were in this class. People who performed the smallest kindness to a heretic fell into it. How could this attitude be reconciled with the teachings of Christ? In the gospel according to St John XIII, 34 and 35, it is written that Jesus said:

'A new commandment I give unto you, That ye love one

another; as I have loved you, that ye also love one another. By this shall all men know that ye are my disciples, if ye have love one to another.'

It is ironical that it should have been a definite sin against the Church to show Christian charity to those in distress. Surely this is an indication of the wide divergence between the Church and the teachings of Jesus. For to obey this commandment of Jesus Christ was a sin according to the Church. What, therefore could that Church possibly have in common with Christ, but the name?

The Inquisitors made themselves responsible for dealing with certain offences outside heresy, but they were much more lenient with regard to these. They would always arrange that the sin they dealt with could be construed as a sin against the Church, thus coming under their jurisdiction.

The cells in the prisons of the Inquisition were of varying degrees of comfort; the best were relegated to those guilty of offences such as bigamy. The second class of cell was slightly less comfortable, and into these were sent the servants of the Inquisition who had failed to carry out their duties in accordance with the commands of their masters; the third type – foul, dank dungeons in which rats and other vermin abounded – were reserved for heretics.

Bigamy was not in itself a sin which the Inquisition wished to punish with any degree of severity. A bigamist who confessed what he had done would be given a very light sentence; if he declared that he had been overcome by passion and so led to marry more than once, that was well enough; it was only if he expressed contempt for marriage itself – which was one of the Church's sacraments – that he came dangerously near to heresy, and a more severe sentence was inflicted.

Adultery and fornication presented difficulties. These were sins in which Popes and priests had indulged riotously. Adultery and fornication, declared the Inquisition, did not come under its jurisdiction unless the adulterers and fornicators expressed the belief that there was no sin in committing them; then, of course, they were setting themselves in opposition to the laws of Holy Church – thus being guilty of heresy.

The laws of the Inquisition had been worked out with the utmost care and it was as though excuses for brutal conduct were continually drawn over the truth by obscure methods of expression and formal procedure.

Ludovico á Paramo declares that God was the first Inquisitor and that in the Book of Genesis He set an example to the Inquisitors to come. Adam and Eve ate of the fruit of the tree of knowledge and thus were guilty of heresy; their punishment was to be turned out of the garden. They lost the Garden of Eden, and clearly says Ludovico à Paramo, God sets the example of confiscation of wordly goods. They wore skins and these were equivalent to the *sanbenito*, that hideous dress which proclaimed man or woman heretic. It was comforting to cite this example, to reassure themselves: We are brutal, we torture our fellow men and women although we fall short of shedding their blood – leaving that to the secular arm – but we are merely following the example laid down for us by God Himself.

The fiery Jehovah of the Old Testament seems to be a God after their own hearts, whereas the teaching of the gentle Jesus of the New, although they called themselves his followers, appeared to be ignored by them. It therefore seems extraordinarily illogical that they should have had such a contempt for the Jewish religion (which Jesus and his family followed devoutly) and looked with loathing on those who reverted to it after being baptized as Christians. Religion, to these people, was largely a matter of eating or not eating pork, sprinkling water or not sprinkling water in mourning chambers, circumcision and such rites. The real teaching of Christ had been choked out of existence in their churches by dogma and ritual.

The *sanbenito* was the garment of shame. Those who wore it did so as a sign that they had sinned, and that they were doing penance for those sins. It had first been brought into existence by St Dominic, but the garment worn by penitents in his day was different from that with which Tomás de Torquemada burdened those whom he ordained should be punished. Its name derives from *saco bendito*, which quickly became *san-*

benito and was often called in Spain the *zamarra*, the sheep-skin jacket of today.

St Dominic decreed that the garment of shame should be of sackcloth and dismal in colour. During the Albigensian war, those who were fighting for the Church wore crosses stitched on their tunics; the cross was the sign of a good Catholic. St Dominic decided however that in order that a penitent should be recognized he should wear two crosses on his garment.

After the war men no longer displayed the crosses and it was decided that two yellow crosses should be used on the *sanbenito* – one on each breast.

Before the days of Torquemada the *sanbenito* was simply a tunic, very similar to those worn by the members of religious orders; but the zealous Inquisitor-General had been quick to see how this garment could provide an additional torture, and decided to use it more frequently than hitherto. The ordinary tunic with the cross was too similar to those worn by holy men. Therefore its shape was changed. It became a loose-fitting garment with a hole in the top that it might be slipped over the head and hung on the body like a tabard. It reached the knees, and was made of yellow sackcloth; the crosses which were sewn to it were blood-red in colour.

The type of *sanbenito* worn by the victim depended on the nature of his sin, and those condemned to wear them were obliged to do so at certain times, accordiing to their sins. Some wore them on Sundays and holy days. Others dared not be seen without them. People began to shrink from contamination with them, for they quickly came to believe that there was evil in the hideous yellow garment.

For the man or woman who was merely suspected of being a heretic there was the *sanbenito* without cross, providing he or she was a suspect *leviter*. If the person were a suspect *vehementer*, the *sanbenito* which was worn was decorated with only one arm of the cross and this was on both back and front of the garment; the suspect *violenter* wore the complete cross.

Men and women were sentenced to wear the *sanbenito* for several years, some sentences including flogging at the church door.

But for those who were found guilty of heresy and condemned to the stake there were the most hideous *sanbenitos* of all. These bore grotesque figures painted on them, and these figures were symbolic of the fate which awaited their wearers. Those who had repented and were attending the *auto de fé* to hear a sentence passed which would be severe enough (such as life imprisonment and confiscation of all worldly goods) wore a *sanbenito* with a cross on back and front, and in addition to this was a tall cap, like a mitre, which was worn by all who had been found guilty of heresy. This was called the *coroza*, and on this would be a complete cross.

The relapsed heretic – who had repented and was condemned to be burned but, as an act of mercy because of his repentance, was to be strangled before the fire touched his body – wore a *sanbenito* decorated with flames and devils with pitchforks prodding these fires; but the flames on this garment pointed downwards, as an indication that the wearer was not to die by the fire but was to be strangled before burning.

The heretic who remained true to his beliefs to the last, and was condemned to be burned alive, wore a *sanbenito* decorated with flames and devils, but flames in his case pointed upwards, which indicated his fate.

Any who confessed their guilt and asked for reconciliation, even when the faggots were about to be lighted, were – in the great mercy of the Church – granted it, and strangled before burning.

It was this *sanbenito* which, the subtle mind of Torquemada enabled him to judge, would be of benefit in his campaign against the heretic.

Many men and women were condemned to the *vergüenza*: that is 'the shame'. This was the sentence passed on those who had been found guilty of heresy and had requested to be reconciled to the Church. Their pleas had been granted but they must of course perform their penance, and this was the one allotted to them.

They must join a procession of similar offenders and in fine weather or foul parade the streets naked from the waist up. At the head of the procession walked the familiars of the Inquisition.

Each penitent carried a green candle, which was unlit; this was another of those affectations so beloved by the members of the Inquisition. It signified that these miserable wretches had not yet 'seen the light', but they were not utterly damned since they were given candles to carry hopefully. When the Church received them they would be allowed to light their candles.

At the Cathedral the procession would halt and, as the half naked men and women passed into the church, two priests would be standing at the doors to mark the sign of the cross on their foreheads, bidding them, as they did so, receive the cross which they had rejected and lost.

In the Cathedral the Inquisitors would be waiting for the penitents, the green cross, symbol of the Inquisition having been hoisted above the altar. The notary would read out the names of the men and women who had come to hear their sentences, and what penance they were to perform.

For this offence it was decreed that for six Fridays in succession, stripped to the waist, their heads and feet bare, they were to walk in procession through the streets as they had on this day. As they walked they would be whipped; and even when this penance was over they would never be allowed to hold any honourable office, nor jewel or fine clothes; and they must give one fifth of their possessions into the keeping of the inquisition, that some grace might come to them, since what was taken from them would be used in the holy war against the Moors of Granada.

There was one grim warning which was always issued. If any of these men and women fell again into error there was no hope for them. Whatever confessions they made they would not be believed; and the Holy Inquisition would have but one alternative in dealing with them. They would be abandoned to the secular law.

Every man or woman who had known the shame of walking almost naked through the streets, who had felt the whip across his or her shoulders, who had felt the press of eager sightseers avid for sensation yet never daring to show pity even if they felt it, also knew that one more slip, one more disgruntled enemy, and theirs would be the fiery death.

An *auto de fé*! The words must have caused a thrill of horror, yet hideous fascination, even among the most insensitive. Those days on which the *autos* were held were the gala days and attracted as many people and produced even more excitement than the traditional bull-fight.

The people must be made to understand the nature of these occasions. They were not entertainments merely, they were religious ceremonies. It was for this reason that they were always held on Sundays or the holy day of the Church.

It was not intended that the day should be marred by riotous revelling. The Inquisitors shuddered to think what might take place if the ceremonies were prolonged into the night. They had visions of men and women, intoxicated by excitement, giving way to sinful acts, and they, who were about to bring to numbers of people the most acute suffering that can be imagined, could not tolerate the thought of the occasions being desecrated by Sin.

Thus it was decided that *autos de fé* should begin in the early morning that they might be over before dusk and so the opportunity to sin would not be given to the spectators, and the Inquisitors and their adherents would have nothing on their immaculate consciences.

On the evening before an *auto de fé* was to take place relaxed heretics were brought to the palace of the Inquisition, and there they were told that the next day they were to be burned alive. In their 'mercy' the Inquisitors allotted each of them two priests who would be their companions throughout the night and who would do their utmost to save their souls; as for their bodies they were past saving; but if they should confess their heresy and declare their great desire for reconciliation with the Church, although they must die for their sins, they should be granted the privilege of strangulation before the flames consumed their bodies.

The next morning they were brought forth from the prison of the Inquisition, all the prisoners arrayed in their *sanbenitos* which denoted their crime, about their necks ropes, which also pinpointed them. The procession was now ready to begin.

First came the bearer of the green cross which was draped

with black material, and immediately behind it were the company of familiars.

The priest who was to celebrate Mass came next, and over him, borne by four men, was a canopy of scarlet and gold. He carried the Host and, as he passed through the crowds, all men, women and children were expected to fall to their knees. With so many members of the Inquisition close at hand none would dare remain standing at such a time, for it was certain that such behaviour would put the culprit into the class of 'suspected heretic'.

More familiars followed, and then came the prisoners in varying degrees of misery – some having the marks of torture upon them, others suffering only shame. With each of the prisoners who was doomed to die by burning were two Dominicans – peguin-like in their white vestments and flowing black hoods. The people in the crowds must be shown how merciful were the Inquisitors, and how even at this late hour it was their urgent desire to save these wretched creatures from being burned alive.

Following the prisoners, and fastened to long green poles, were effigies of people who had been found guilty of heresy and had had the good fortune to escape from Spain. Their faces were painted with hideous grimaces, and the yellow *sanbenitos* (flames, fanned by devils, pointing upwards) had been on the figures together with the *crozas*. Here also were the bodies, which had been dug up from the graves, of those who had been condemned as heretics after they had died. This must have been the most ghastly if not the most pitiable section of the procession.

Now came the Inquisitors, banners of red sarcenet carried before them; on one side of the banners were emblazoned the Papal arms entwined with those of Ferdinand and Isabella, and on the other the arms of the Inquisition.

The *alguazils* and minor officials followed and on either side of the procession marched soldiers with halberds on their shoulders.

Straggling in the rear came the sightseers all making their way to the Cathedral Square (some eager to view the spectacle, some afraid to stay away) to await the supreme excitement which would culminate on the *quemadero*.

The Inquisition had always worked with the utmost formality, and although the sentences of these poor people had already been decided on, each must be called before a tribunal and listen to the list of his crimes; and as there was a sermon to be preached, and often several hundred victims to be individually accused, the ceremony continued for many hours. There were occasions when an *auto de fé* began at six in the morning of a summer's day and lasted until dusk. As the final scene was the burning, this meant that, in addition to the exquisite agony of the torture chamber, the sufferers were given the mental torture which such an occasion must have inflicted.

In a great square of the town in which the *auto* was being held — usually the Cathedral Square — platforms were set up and decorated with black crêpe. On these platforms benches had been arranged, tier on tier, and here the prisoners were forced to sit so that the crowds might see them and, to show what good Catholics they were, shout insults at them, and inflict minor indignities and pain, such as setting fire to their beards — a pastime which was lightheartedly called by the mob 'Shaving the New Christians'. On the benches with the prisoners were the friars, who continued to exhort them to confess ... an outward sign of the merciful nature of the Inquisition; and all about the platform were set up the long poles with the grotesque straw figures in *senbenitos* and the desecrated decomposing bodies dragged from their graves.

On a second platform the Inquisitors and their servants took their seats; on this platform a black-draped green cross stood, with an altar lighted by candles. Incense burned on this platform and no doubt it was necessary.

Mass was thus celebrated and the sermon was preached; this was usually of great length and, when it was over, the Grand Inquisitor rose and lifting his arms declaimed the oath of allegiance to the Inquisition; this the crowd must repeat after him; they must fall to their knees and swear that they would defend the Holy Office against all who came against it; they swore they would be faithful to it in life and in death; they would not flinch, whatever it should ask of them; they would pluck out their right eye or cut off their right hand and give their life itself if the Inquisition demanded it of them.

When the sovereigns were present at this ceremony they refrained from repeating the oath, for Isabella and Ferdinand had always determined that Spain should not rest under the domination of the Papacy; and it would never be forgotten that this organization had its roots in Rome, for its purpose was to maintain the Catholic Faith, the headquarters of which was the Vatican. The Emperor Charles never swore the oath of allegiance to the Inquisition; it was Charles's son, Philip, who was the first sovereign to do so. Philip, the strange and morose hermit, the fervent and zealous Catholic, took the oath often and was seen by his subjects rising to his feet, his sword held high, swearing to serve the Inquisition.

Now came the farce of abandoning the prisoners to the secular arm. The Church had done all she could; she could not save their souls, and that was her only concern. There was nothing for her to do but hand them over to the law, that the punishment for heresy might be carried out.

This was followed by reading a detailed account of the crimes of each person condemned – from those who were to receive the lightest penance to those who were to be burned alive. The latter of course were kept to the last – *the pièce de résistance.*

From the altar a spurious appeal was made to the secular arm to show mercy: surely the most despicable moment of the whole wicked proceedings. Let the secular arm deal with them in such a manner that blood would not be shed. Well, if they were burned alive, blood would not be shed. And even if anyone put a different construction on the phrase, the Inquisition was blameless; it had merely despaired of saving their obstinate souls; it was not concerned with what happened to their bodies.

In a field was the *quemadero* – the place of fire. The stakes were set up and at the foot of these the faggots were piled.

Those who had become reconciled to the Church, although they were relapsed heretics, were given the benefit of strangulation as the faggots were lighted. Many at the last dreadful moment naturally cried out that they wished for reconciliation, the quick death of strangulation being so much more preferable to the hideous pain of being burned alive.

The people shout their approval; the Inquisitors sit, hands folded, deeply shocked by all the wickedness in the world, serene in their own virtue, in bringing about justice, so clever that – although they have brought those groaning, fainting men and women to this horror – because they abandoned them in time to the secular arm, there is no blood on their hands. A pall of smoke hangs over the *quemadero*; the air is filled with the smell of roasting human flesh.

It is more exciting than a bull-fight, for it is much more thrilling to see a human being suffer than an animal; the long ceremony, the chanting of monks, the tolling of bells, the smell of incense, the holiness of the proceedings has a comforting effect. All has been sanctified by these things.

There would be a feeling too of exultation, and because it was vaguely tinged with apprehension it would be the more exciting for that. The Inquisitors were indefatigable. This *auto* was at an end, but before long there would be another. Scarcely four weeks separated one *auto* from another.

When would the next pall of smoke rise above the field which had become the *quemadero*? When would they again have such fun, throwing refuse at the prisoners and burning their beards? When would they hear again those cries of anguish? And who would be the next victims?

These were the questions which made the spectators pause and shiver. Who could tell? The Inquisition was more than two centuries old; but until now it had been as an infant struggling for life.

This was the new Inquisition. The Spanish Inquisition. Torquemada's Inquisition.

That was why many in the crowd, even those as humble and insignificant as muleteers or water-carriers, asked themselves Who next?

CHAPTER TEN

THE MYSTERIOUS AFFAIR
AT LA GUARDIA

The foremost ambition of Ferdinand – if not of Isabella – was to conquer the whole of Spain and demolish the last Moorish stronghold. The Moors were a warlike people and a desperate one for during the 1480s their position was growing more and more precarious.

It may have been due to this rooted preoccupation of the sovereigns that Torquemada was allowed to continue in such power. Next to the sovereigns themselves he was the most powerful man in Spain, and because of his fiery eloquence and his aura of sanctity he was on occasions able to dominate even them.

In addition to making war on the Moors the sovereigns had anxieties within their own kingdom. In 1484 a marriage was proposed between Catharine the young Queen of Navarre and Jean d'Albret, a nobleman of France. The sovereigns naturally saw the danger to Spain of such a union for the d'Albret estates were on the border of Navarre, and the French had long been casting covetous eyes on the province. A French King of Navarre naturally would cause some anxiety to Isabella and Ferdinand.

Unfortunately for them, Catharine's mother was a Frenchwoman determined to further the match with Jean d'Albret, and in spite of their efforts to prevent it, the marriage took place.

However all was not peace in Navarre for a large proportion of the people had no wish to be overpowered by French influence; and Ferdinand, with sly diplomacy, came to an understanding with the discontented Navarrese that, should the French seek advantage from the situation, he and they would prevent its being taken.

This created an uneasy situation on the borders of Aragon and here was at least one trouble spot to occupy the thoughts of the Spanish Sovereigns, so that they were obliged to leave the management of certain home affairs to those ministers whom they considered trustworthy. And who, in the eyes of Isabella and Ferdinand, could be more worthy than Tomàs de Torquemada? They knew that the Dominican had the interests of Spain at heart, yet at the same time the very nature of his office meant that he must be influenced by Rome.

Isabella, sternly insisting that she would dominate in Castile, had brought law and order to her dominion in a manner which was admirable. It had been no easy matter to subdue her unruly subjects who, accustomed to the anarchy which had prevailed during the reigns of her father and brother, at first were very reluctant to tolerate restraint. She insisted that the nobles, who had in the past settled their disputes with one another by force of arms, must submit to legal arbitration; and she was rapidly eliminating the bandits of the country by making great efforts to capture them, and, when they were in her hands, inflicting severe punishment.

Although she would always listen to Torquemada and paid him the utmost respect, she adhered to her determination to remain supreme ruler even if this meant coming into conflict with the Church. This is clearly shown by an incident which occurred in Truxillo in the year 1486. A priest of the town had been found guilty of a minor offence and sent to prison by the secular authorities. The ecclesiastical community always jealous of their authority were incensed that the civil law should take the judgment out of their hands. The misconduct of a priest they maintained, was their affair, even if the priest had committed some offence which was in no way connected with his ecclesiastical duties. They therefore demanded that the priest be handed over to the Church that they might deal with him. This request was refused by the civic magistrate.

It was very easy for priests in the various pulpits to inflame the people; and it is not difficult to understand that, living in the grim shadow of the Inquisition, they were always more than eager to show their respect for the Church. Moreover, the mob was always ready to be inflamed. Raiding and pillaging were profitable, particularly when the approval of the Church and the Inquisition could be gained by indulging in them.

As a result of the promptings of the priests, the mob of Truxillo rose in a body, stormed the jail in which the priest was being held, and freed not only him but the other prisoners.

The ecclesiastical community folded it hands and smiled. This would be a lesson to the secular law, to leave churchmen to be dealt with by the Church. But the strong-minded Isabella was not to be intimidated. She had her own views on what was right or wrong, and devout supporter of the Church though she might be, she was determined to maintain the authority of civil law. She therefore sent her soldiers to Truxillo, where they were to restore order and arrest the ringleaders of the mob which had stormed the prison.

These were sentenced to death and the priests whose preaching had incited the mob were banished from Spain. This was Isabella's answer to the Church. It had her support within limits but the state was supreme.

The establishment of the Inquisition in Castile under the guidance of Tomás de Torquemada was proving very successful and Ferdinand was delighted. Much wealth was pouring into the exchequer, and he was sure that Torquemada's zeal would be one of the principal means of bringing about the downfall of the Moors.

The Inquisition in Aragon on the other hand was a feeble institution compared with that of Castile. It was a hundred years or so since it had been established in Aragon and the people there had never greatly objected to it, the reason being that its rule was slack; it was even tolerant, following the same course as in other countries where it was dying a lingering death.

Ferdinand needed money for his war; Isabella wished to see all Spain united under Catholic sway, and quite clearly there was one way of attaining both objects. Torquemada's instructions must be obeyed in Aragon as in Castile; Torquemada's Inquisition must replace the lackadaisical method of the last hundred years.

In April of the year 1484 the Cortes assembled at

Taraçona, and Ferdinand, who presided over it had taken Torquemada with him. He announced his intention of adjusting the Inquisition of Aragon that it might fall into line with that of Castile, and he introduced Tomás de Torquemada as the Inquisitor-General of Aragon.

The Aragonese were dismayed, for stories of the terrible sights to be seen at the Castilian *autos de fé* had travelled as far as Aragon. The new Christians trembled; and the richer they were, the more they trembled. They knew that Ferdinand's greedy hands were itching to seize their treasures, and when they looked at the gaunt, pitiless face of the Prior of the Holy Cross, Tomás de Torquemada, they would have known – even if his reputation had not travelled before him – that they could hope for little mercy.

But they did not altogether despair. They had *heard* of the horrors which had been taking place in Castile, and that was different from seeing them actually taking place; they must have thought that the Castilians were a little foolish to be as meek as they were, and that they, the Aragonese, would in such dire emergency show a little more spirit.

The usual orders were issued to the populace, the formula taking the same shape as so recently in Castile. Everyone was to help the officers of the Inquisition or be suspected of heresy; and Torquemada lost no time in appointing two Inquisitors – Pedro Arbués de Epila, who was a Canon of the Metropolitan Church of Saragossa, and Fray Gaspar Juglar, a Dominican monk.

Even when these two men had been appointed, the wealthy New Christians of Aragon still did not believe that they could be forced to live under the same reign of terror as that which prevailed in Castile, and two deputations were despatched – one to the Pope, one to Ferdinand. They asked that they might continue with the old customs and that the new instructions of Torquemada might not immediately apply to Aragon. These two requests were ignored; and the new Inquisitors went to work with a zeal worthy of their master.

The results of their labours were the *autos de fé* of May and June 1485; and when the despairing people of Saragossa saw their friends in the hideous *sanbenitos* taking part in the grim processions, and witnessed the burning alive of several people, they grew sullen.

Before the second of the *autos* had taken place Inquisitor Gaspar Juglar was stricken by a mysterious illness; he died of this during May, and it was generally believed that he had been poisoned.

One consequence of this was an increase in the activities of the Inquisitors, but a certain note of fear had been struck, and Pedro Arbués was nervous. He carefully tested all he ate and drank, never moved without a bodyguard and wore armour beneath his habit; he even wore a steel cap hidden by his hood.

When Leonardo Eli, one of the richest New Christians in Saragossa, was arrested, those who had believed that through their wealth and influence they could, by presenting petitions, put a stop to the reign of terror, realized that they had been mistaken. However they did not mean to give up easily, and one of the wealthiest and most influential of the community, a *converso* named Juan Pedro Sanchez, called together a little group of men in similar position to his own (including his four brothers who held important government posts) and a plan was formulated.

The meetings were held at the house of a certain Luis de Santangel who held high position under Ferdinand, and here they agreed that there was one way – and one way only – of making known their determination to turn Torquemada's Inquisition out of Aragon. They had witnessed the horrible deaths of certain of their friends; they must employ drastic remedies; nothing could be effective but the death of the Inquisitor Pedro Arbués. If he were assassinated, another would be reluctant to take his place and it would be realized that the people of Aragon could not be treated as the Castilians had been.

One of their number must perform the deed and as a reward the slayer would receive 500 florins. Six men offered themselves for the task; one of these was Juan de Esperandeu who had special reasons for wishing to strike the blow. His father had been arrested and was, at the time of the conspiracy, in the prison of the Inquisition, and so far as the son knew, suffering in the torture chambers.

Pedro Arbués, if he had no knowledge of the conspiracy, was aware of his unpopularity; after the death of his fellow Inquisitor he took so many precautions against assassination that again and again the conspirators found themselves foiled.

They grew more and more restive and at length decided on a daring plan. They knew that Arbués must visit the Metropolitian Church for midnight service, and they decided that, since they could catch him nowhere else, they would do so there. They hid themselves in the church and waited.

It was not difficult to conceal themselves in the dimly lighted church. They knew that Arbués would enter from the cloisters and had to traverse the dim church to reach the Dominicans in the choir. Even for that short journey he came armed. He carried a stout stick in his hand, beneath his robes was the suit of armour, and his cap was lined with steel. In his other hand was a lantern, and as he came he peered anxiously about him. Before joining the choir however he must kneel in prayer, and to do this it was necessary to set down his stick and lantern. This was what the conspirators had waited for. The singing of the choir was an advantage since they were able to creep up on the kneeling figure without being heard. Esperandeu, no doubt allowing his anguish for his father to blind his judgment, used his sword wildly and merely wounded Arbués in the arm. But his friends came into the attack. Arbués was struck on the head with such force that the steel cap was dented, and a sword pierced a vein in his neck. Arbués struggled to his feet, but Esperandeu, not to be robbed of his revenge, found a vulnerable spot in the armour and drove his sword through the Dominican's body.

The assassins made their escape, for now those who had been singing in the choir realized that all was not well and came running to the fallen man to discover what had happened.

Arbués lived two more days and nights, and died on 17th September, 1485.

The day following the attack, when the news of it had spread through the town, the people gathered in the streets shouting for reprisals on the New Christians. The affair had had the opposite effect to the which had been intended. Instead of arousing the people against the Inquisition it aroused them against that old whipping boy: Jewry.

It was apparent that serious riots were imminent; this is what would have occurred had not Ferdinand's natural son, a young man of seventeen whom his father had already made Archbishop of Saragossa, happened to be in Saragossa at this time. Taking the high officials of his retinue with him he rode into the streets and faced the mob. He advised them against riots, which might not bring retribution to the true perpetrators of the crime and could result in disaster to themselves; let them go quietly to their homes; he would promise them that justice should be done.

Torquemada at once sent three new Inquisitors (Fr Juan Colvera, Pedro de Monterubio, and Alonso de Alarcon) to the town to replace Arbués and Juglar; and the officers of the Inquisition left their old building and established themselves in the royal alcazar, the Castle of Aljaferia, where they were protected by guards. Not that they were in need of this protection; but, although Torquemada was pleased that Ferdinand's young son had prevented rioting, he wished to sustain the anger of the people of Saragossa against the New Christians.

Arrests were made; the torturers were soon working full time in the dismal chambers; it was not long before men and women were being brought in to testify against those who had conspired to kill the Inquisitors of Saragossa.

Juan Pedro Sanchez was fortunate enough to escape from Spain. His effigy was burned at an *auto de fé* with the live bodies of others who had taken part in the plot. Esperandeu was caught; his punishment was to be put on a hurdle and dragged through the streets to the Cathedral, on the steps of which he was taken from the hurdle that the hands which had struck the blows at Aryués might be cut off. After that he was hanged, taken down alive, castrated and quartered.

The hopes of the conspirators had failed to materialize. The people of Saragossa, out of hatred of the New Christians, or perhaps in the hope of a little loot, had given their approval to the setting-up of the Inquisition in Aragon.

Autos de fé began to take place regularly in Aragon as they had in Castile; and determined to show the people that they must submit to its decrees, the Inquisitors increased their harshness. They wished the people to understand the power of this organisation, and when one, a New Christian, realizing that none of his sect was safe in Aragon, escaped and took refuge in Navarre with the Infante Jaime, the latter, though he was the son of the Queen of Navarre, was arrested and brought before the Inquisitors.

He was accused of hindering the activities of the Holy Office and, as all knew, any who did this were suspected of heresy. Jaime was found guilty of this sin against the Church; he was put in prison and sentenced to be whipped, not through the streets – this might have been too much for the royal family to overlook – but round the church; and as an additional insult, his bastard cousin (Alfonso of Aragon who had been responsible for quelling the mob) should witness his discomfiture.

This should show the power of the Inquisition; this should warn the people against the folly of attempting to subdue the mighty Holy Office.

Nor were they satisfied with the humiliation of the Infante Jaime. Another of the conspirators, Gaspar de Santa Cruz, who escaped to Toulouse and whose effigy was burned at the *auto de fé*, died before the Inquisitors could bring him back to Spain. His son who had helped his escape, was arrested, and his penance was to go at once to Toulouse, dig up the remains of his father, and there, arrayed in *sanbenito*, burn in public his father's body. To avoid being burned alive himself the young man did this.

As for Pedro Arbués, he was now regarded as a saint, and legends sprang up regarding him. The bells were said to have rung of their own accord the moment he died, and twelve days after his blood had been shed it was said (after it was too late to put this to the test) that it was still warm and wet on the stones of the church, and a handkerchief dipped therein would be stained red and provide a holy relic. He was buried in the church beneath that very spot where he had been struck down, and a monument was erected to him. He was beatified in the 17th century by Alexander VII, and canonized in the 19th by Pius IX. But perhaps his chief claim to notice (among those who see the Inquisition as a blot on civilization and an Institution which did great disservice to Christianity) is that his death was of significance in the history of the Inquisition. Had the people of Aragon forgotten their enmity towards the Jews, had they stood with them against the Inquisition, they could at that time have prevented its growth; they could have asserted their own right to freedom of thought. And if Aragon had taken that turning at that precise time, Castile would surely have followed; and the Inquisition could have become a feeble plant which struggled for a while and withered away, as it had in other European countries.

The great persecution came to a climax in the year 1490, the beginning of that decade which surely was the most momentous in Spanish history: the year 1492 stands out as of greatest significance, for during it Christopher Columbus discovered America, Torquemada expelled the Jews from Spain, and Ferdinand and Isabella drove the Moors from Granada and the reconquest of Spain was completed.

It was in the year 1490 that an event took place which undoubtedly hastened the completion of one of these events; that is the expulsion of the Jews.

This began without apparent significance when a New Christian named Benito Garcia made a journey in the course of his business. As he was a woolcomber his trade made it necessary for him to travel from place to place in order to buy and sell his goods; and on one of these journeys he had the misfortune to stay the night at a small inn in the village of Astorga.

There were a great many people staying at the inn that night, and Garcia could not be given a room to himself; so he was forced to share one with a party of men.

These men were far from honest and, noticing the good clothes of their room-mate, they conspired to rob him while he slept.

As soon as he was asleep they took his knapsack, opened it and began quarrelling over its contents. However they were quickly subdued by a discovery they made. In the knapsack was a wafer, and the fact that it was in the possession of a layman, who being a Jew must have stolen it, meant that a great sin had been committed against the Church.

Like the Guzman who had entered the house of a New Christian in order to seduce his daughter, these robbers at once forgot their own crime in the immensity of the one they believed they had uncovered. They fell upon Garcia and insisted that he accompany them without delay to the magistrate.

This magistrate was Dr Pedro de Villada who had worked often with the Inquisition and had, unluckily for Garcia, been promised that before long he would be raised to the position of Inquisitor. He was therefore determined to show his mettle, and Benito Barcia seemed to offer him a good opportunity of doing this.

He demanded that Garcia admit he was guilty of practising the rites of Judaism, and that he had stolen the wafer for an evil purpose.

Garcia was terrified. He guessed of what he would be accused, for there had been circulated in recent years many stories of Jewish practices, and again and again they were accused of partaking in ritual murder. This, it was alleged, usually took the form of kidnapping a Christian boy and crucifying him; and for this ceremony consecrated Hosts were said to be stolen from the Christian churches.

He insisted on his innocence, whereupon Pedro de Villada ordered that he be given two hundred lashes as a beginning, and when Garcia continued to protest his innocence, the water torture was applied.

During his terrible suffering the poor man broke down and admitted all that was required of him. Yes, he had been baptized; he was a New Christian; and he had relapsed into Judaism. That was not enough; he must incriminate others.

He thereupon explained that, five years before, he had met a New Christian named Juan de Ocaña; this man practised Judaism and advised Garcia to do the same, but to do so with craft; and in this Garcia had followed the advice of Ocaña; he had returned to Judaism in secret although he had forced his children to go to the Christian church lest by not doing so they should call suspicion on to himself. He had fabricated 'confessions' which he made to the priest, and he made a mockery of the communion; in secret he spat on the Viaticum.

In addition to Ocaña he mentioned the names of Mosé and

Yucé Franco and their father Ça Franco. He visited this family in the course of business and he knew them to be Judaizers because he ate meat on Fridays at their home.

Villada immediately arrested Ocaña, Ça Franco, who was eighty, and his son Yucé who was only twenty. Fortunately for Mosé he died before he could be arrested.

They were then taken to the prison at Segovia which had at one time been the residence of the Queen's lady-in-waiting and intimate friend, Beatriz de Bobadilla; while they were there Yucé fell ill, and as he did not expect to live to stand further trial and condemnation he boldly asked for a Jewish physician to be sent to him that he might talk to him in his own language, and a Rabbi to pray with him.

This was an opportunity too good to be missed. The Inquisitors declared they could not refuse the request of a dying man. They therefore sent one of their spies with instructions to show great sympathy for the young man and at the same time make him divulge the names of others who had shared in his heretical practices.

The physician arrived, and with him came the Dominican, Alonso Enriquez, disguised as the Rabbi Abraham. He showered sympathy on the young man, and Yucé completely duped was greatly comforted.

It would do him good to talk, he was told; his comforter would like to know for what reason he had been arrested.

Yucé, who must have heard that the wafer had been discovered, replied that he had been arrested for being concerned in the ritual murder of a Christian boy.

This was a startling revelation, for although it was the sight of the wafer in Garcia's knapsack which had in the first place made the robbers drag him before Villada, this was the first time ritual murder had been mentioned.

Villada immediately realized the importance of the case on his hands. It was clearly no ordinary affair of New Christians turning back to their own religion. He sent Enriquez once more to talk to Yucé, but the young man had recovered his health a little and with it his sense. He refused to say any more.

The case was then taken to the highest authority – to Torquemada himself. Torquemada was delighted. He had long been seeking an excuse to drive all Jews out of Spain, and a case of ritual murder, which could actually be substantiated to the satisfaction of the excitable and superstitious people of Spain, was exactly what he needed. If he could make Ferdinand and Isabella realize the harm the Jews were doing in Spain and at the same time rouse the wrath of the people, he had no doubt that before long he could bring about that for which he had been working during the greater part of his life.

He therefore decided that the case should have his personal supervision.

Meanwhile Yucé, under examination, had admitted that he had gone to La Guardia three years before to buy wheat from a family of millers there. There were four brothers in this family. (It is rather confusing that they should have the same name as Yucé, but although they were Francos they were not related.) It was easy to understand how during the business deal the conversation turned to the making of unleavened bread and the passover. They also, Yucé continued, talked of other Jewish customs, and the brothers told him that one Good Friday they had stolen a young Christian boy and crucified him in the way Jesus of Nazareth had been crucified.

After making this extraordinary announcement, Yucé was left alone for three months. The suspense he endured during that time – when he would have realized the extent to which he had incriminated himself and others – must have been unnerving. It was exactly the effect the Inquisitors wished to create.

Yucé was not brought for trial until the following December. The year was 1490.

The first accusation brought against Yucé was that he had believed Christianity to be false and had tried to attract Christians to his religion.

Then came the important charge. He was accused of associating with men who had crucified a young Christian boy on a certain Good Friday.

He was also charged with having stolen a consecrated Host

that it might be used for sorcery and mockery of Jesus Christ, and with other offences against the law of the Inquisition, which would be dealt with at a later date.

Yucé, who at this time had no idea that the man to whom he had talked of the crucifixion was any but the Rabbi Abraham, declared that the accusation was the greatest of falsehoods.

He was allowed a counsel for the defence and the lawyer Bachelor Sanc and the advocate Juan de Pantigosa were allowed to plead for him.

Sanc enthusiastically defended his client, declaring that the accusations were quite vague and, before they could condemn him on such flimsy evidence, the prosecution must be more precise concerning the people who had shared in his so-called guilt and the time when the offences were committed. Such vagueness might be permissible when the Inquisition was dealing with heretics, but Yucé Franco was not a heretic. He was a Jew who, as such, could not be treated as a heretic. Moreover Yucé was an uneducated boy, a cobbler by trade. How could one so lacking in education attempt to convert people to Judaism? Sanc demanded that his client be given his freedom.

The court then declared that thirty days should be allowed to the prosecution to prove the charges against Yucé. But in thirty days the prosecution had been unable to prove its case, yet Yucé was kept in prison.

The young boy was nearly driven insane by solitary confinement and ignorance as to what was going on. There was one thing for which he was grateful, and that was the kindness of his jailor, who brought him a guitar that he might strum on it to make the long hours pass more quickly.

One day, about three months after his appearance in court, he was playing the guitar when he heard a voice. It was that of Benito, who had been placed in the cell below him. There was a crack in the floor, which had been made by the jailors for this very purpose, but Yucé had no idea of this.

It was necessary for the two men to talk rather loudly to make themselves heard by one another; and notaries were outside the doors of their cells taking down all that was said.

So they talked together, Benito telling Yucé that his father had been arrested, how he had been tortured and during the process had given enough away to send him to the stake. Benito asked if Yucé had a needle – or a knife would do. He wished to destroy evidence of his circumcision. Yucé replied that he would die if he tried such a trick, to which Benito retorted that he would prefer to die that way than to be burned alive.

Yucé's great concern was about the wafer because he, as a Jew, could not be tried for heresy. He asked Benito about his arrest and that of his own father; then he wanted to know how much had been discovered about the wafer.

Benito could tell him little about that; he went on to curse the day when he had abandoned the law of Moses for the Christian Faith. He had not only been baptized and accepted Christianity, he complained, but had given a water font to the church; his reward had been to be given the water torture. He would die a Jew he declared; they could burn him alive but he would be true to the old faith.

Having recorded all these remarks which had passed between the two prisoners, the Inquisitors had Yucé brought once more before them.

Under the fatigue of continual questioning Yucé told them that he had heard from a Jewish physician that Benito Garcia had been commanded by his brethren to steal a consecrated Host, and that he had got possession of the keys of the Church of La Guardia and had stolen the Host. He had been suspected and sent to prison for two days, but as nothing was proved against him he was released. Yucé believed that Benito's friends wished to use the Host for some Jewish rite.

The Inquisitors felt that they were making some progress, and again Yucé was brought up for questioning and again after some weary hours he was communicative.

From consecrated Hosts, Jews could make charms which could protect them from Christians. Thus spoke Yucé. His brother Mosé, who had since died, had together with the four millers procured a Host and made this charm.

Again there was a session of questioning and Yucé remembered that the spell had been created in a cave outside the village of La Guardia. Later he admitted that the spell was made with something besides the Host. This was a heart – the heart of a Christian boy.

There were long intervals between the examination of Yucé, and there is no doubt that in this the Inquisitors were adhering to the rules set out by Eymeric and acknowledged to be good by Torquemada. They were submitting the boy to the agony of suspense, for all this time he had no notion as to what was happening to his fellow conspirators.

At length he declared he would tell all he knew, on one condition. They had imprisoned his father; and his condition was that he and the old man should be pardoned.

He should be pardoned, said the Inquisitors, providing Yucé told everything he knew. Yucé then said that he had not confessed before owing to a pact he had made with the others not to confess anything until a year had passed.

All those who were now prisoners, he went on, had met one night in the cave of which he had already told them; and he saw there a Host and a human heart. A spell was made which was supposed to protect them against the Inquisition.

Whose was the heart? asked the Inquisitors.

He had been told, Yucé replied, that it had been taken from a Christian boy whom the others had crucified.

The Inquisitors were delighted. This was exactly what, for all these months, they had been working so hard to get.

They then decided that they would bring the old man Ça Franco up for questioning, letting him know that his son had betrayed the conspirators.

The old man, terrified by the subtle threats of torture, began to talk, telling them even more that Yucé had betrayed. Yes, there had been a stolen Host; there had been a human heart; the boy had been whipped and crowned with thorns and crucified there in the cave before the eyes of them all, although he, Ça, had done nothing but look on; as for Yucé, all he had done was to give the boy a little push.

Both Yucé and his father sought to protect each other. Yucé reminded the Inquisitors that his father was a very old man whose sight was failing, and could not have seen clearly what was going on in the cave.

Now the Inquisitors had a case of ritual murder to present to Torquemada, and the Prior of the Holy Cross could lay these facts before the Queen and the country, and so make every Christian rise in fury against the Jews.

It had taken nine months – not thirty days – to collect the evidence, but it had been well worth the trouble.

The court re-opened in October. Sanc put up a good defence and the trial was conducted with the utmost fairness, for Torquemada believed that he had the evidence now to condemn all these men as guilty of the brutal murder of a Christian boy, and he wanted no slur cast on the proceedings. Yucé, however, refused to confirm the confession he had made and, as a result of this, he was taken to the torture chamber where it was planned to give him the water torture.

Seeing the terrible instrument waiting for him, feeling the cords cutting into his wrists and ankles, Yucé shouted that he would confess all.

He then explained that the child had been kidnapped by Juan Franco, who had offered him sweetmeats and taken him to the cave. He confirmed his confession later, so terrified was he of being taken once more to the torture chamber.

Yucé's eighty-year-old father was tortured at the same time as Juan Franco, and they both made confessions which were similar to that of Yucé.

Sanc now saw that he dared not remain in the case, so withdrew. The men were found guilty and were to be abandoned to the secular law.

An *auto de fé* was held, and they all appeared in their *sanbenitos*. Three of the *conversos*, Juan Franco, Juan de Ocaña and Benito Garcia, declared their desire to return to the Catholic Faith when they saw the faggots under them; and before the fires were lighted they were strangled.

Ça and Yucé, however, showed great courage. They were Jews, they declared, and had never been anything else; they would remain faithful to the laws of Moses until they breathed their last.

These two were then bound to the stake and the flesh of their arms and thighs was torn with red hot pincers, for it was felt that they were too evil to be allowed the comparatively quick death by fire. Then, as they writhed in their agony, the faggots were dampened that they might not burn too quickly.

So the old man of eighty and his young son were roasted alive over slow fires.

Thus the famous La Guardia trial which was to have such repercussions throughout Spain.

There are many people who think that the murder of the child never took place at all, and that the confessions extorted under torture or threat were put into the mouths of the sufferers by those men who saw the possibilities which such a case could provide.

It is a fact that one of the men under torture said that the child had been buried in a certain spot, yet when a search was made there no body or remains were found.

A legend naturally grew around the child. This was that a party of Jews had determined on the destruction of Christianity and that the Law of Moses should be set up in its place. To bring about this state of affairs they needed to make a spell, and for this spell they needed two ingredients: a consecrated Host and the heart of a Christian child. These were to be burned to ashes which, when thrown into wells and rivers, would poison the water, with the result that all Christians who drank of it would die insane.

These Jews approached some Christian parents who were very poor and had a great many children; they offered a large sum of money for the heart of one of the children. The mother came to terms with the Jews but, instead of giving the heart of one of her children, handed over a pig's heart.

The Jews proceeded with their experiment, which proved useless. Therefore they determined that next time they would make sure they had the right ingredient by kidnapping a boy and, to ensure that the spell would be effective, crucifying him after the manner in which Jesus Christ had been crucified.

They found a beautiful four-year-old boy in the doorway of a church, gave him sweets and kidnapped him. He was taken to a cave by night and given five thousand strokes with a whip. The little boy, runs the legend, bore the beating with great serenity, but suddenly began to cry. This was when the number of strokes had reached five thousand.

He was asked why he cried, and astonishingly answered that he cried because they had given him five more lashes than His Saviour had received.

He was crowned with thorns and a knife thrust into his side to enable the Jews to fumble for his heart. They had some difficulty in finding this and the child calmly told them how to extract it!

He was then nailed to a cross.

He was known to Christians as Santo Niño; it was said that he was a holy child who was taken straight up to Heaven (for the body of the child, as already mentioned, could not be found) and miracles began to be performed which were credited to him.

It was also said that he had a blind mother who miraculously recovered her sight at the very moment when Santo Niño died.

Whether or not a young boy was crucified in the cave outside La Guardia must remain a mystery, but there is no doubt of the effect of the story on the persecuted people.

Torquemada had the material he needed. His instructions were that an account of the case, in all it hideous detail, should be read from every pulpit in the country. This was done.

Torquemada now awaited results.

He was not disappointed. All over the country the people stirred to action. The worst anti-Jewish riots of the century were threatened.

Torquemada knew that the time had come to put into action his great plan for the expulsion of the Jews.

CHAPTER ELEVEN

THE *MORISCOS*

Meanwhile Ferdinand and Isabella were deeply concerned with operations against the Moors.

In 1487 Ferdinand had left the city of Cordova to launch an attack against Velez Malaga, a town which stood guarding the greater prize of Malaga – and Malaga was only second in importance of Granada, the capital.

The Moors were fierce warriors and, seeing such an array of Christian forces preparing to swoop on them, were determined to put up a brave fight; but foolishly they were quarrelling among themselves, and Boabdil (Abdallah) was on uneasy terms with his father Muley Abul Hacen and his uncle (also named Abdallah but known as El Zagal, or The Valiant).

Ferdinand was full of energy, and behaved with what was considered by his followers as reckless bravery; they often implored him not to endanger his person, to which he made the remark: 'I cannot pause to consider my chances when my subjects are risking their lives for my sake.' His bravery, his determination to lead his men into battle, sharing their risks, made him very popular in the army. And eventually Velez fell to him, and Malaga lay before him, the next goal.

This was one of the richest cities in Moorish Spain. Oranges, pomegranates and olives grew in profusion there and, open to the sea as it was, it enjoyed a brisk trade; the wealth of the inhabitants was apparent in the buildings they had erected; the beautiful gardens were full of flowers and decorated with sparkling fountains.

It was no easy matter to take Malaga, for the Moors had determined at all costs to defend such a prize. Its natural position, protected as it was by the Sierras, was formidable enough, but the Moors had built a great citadel which was connected by a covered passage with another fortress; and a great wall encircled the city except where it sloped to the sea.

News however reached Ferdinand that the rich merchants of Malaga favoured immediate surrender in order to preserve their property, and the King decided to open negotiations with the commander, Hamet Zeli. Hamet Zeli rejected the offer, declaring that he had been commanded by his King to protect Malaga at all cost, and that he was going to do so.

The siege of Malaga had begun. It was to last more than three months, during which the armies of Ferdinand were to undergo many hardships. There were difficulties in transporting water, and plague broke out in nearby villages, which sent a shiver of alarm through the armies. Isabella joined Ferdinand in the camp; a clever move, as the presence of the Queen brought new enthusiasm to the flagging spirits of the soldiers and, instead of grumbling among themselves, the men sought to outdo each other in acts of bravery that they might win the commendation of Isabella and her ladies.

At this time it was debatable whether the armies of Ferdinand and Isabella could take the port of Malaga which was all-important to Granada; the Moors were fanatical in their determination to hold the city for they had lived so long in Spain that they were fighting for their homeland. However the city was lost not so much by force of arms as through those dissensions within the Moorish stronghold; Aragon and Castile, Ferdinand and Isabella, stood together, united.

Muley Hacen and his son Boabdil were quarrelling; while Muley and his brother El Zagal stood together against the young man. Boabdil did all in his power to frustrate his uncle El Zagal, and it is rumoured that he was guilty of poisoning Muley Hacen, his own father. This discord was at the root of the collapse at Malaga and, in conjunction with Ferdinand's armies, brought disaster.

On his side Ferdinand had the wonderful works of his master of ordnance, Francisco Ramirez, whose skill no doubt helped to shorten the siege of Malaga. Ferdinand evidently thought so, for he knighted Francisco. It is said that in this siege gunpowder was used for the first time in European warfare; and under the direction of the clever Ramirez it was very effective.

Meanwhile in the city people were dying in the streets from starvation; and Hamet Zeli, who realized they could no longer hold out, withdrew his soldiers and left the citizens to make the best terms they could with the conquerors.

One of the most important of the merchants, Ali Dordux, sought to make terms of surrender, but at this request Ferdinand merely laughed, remarking that it was a little late in the day for such a conference; it should have taken place three months earlier; now it was for him to dictate terms, not discuss them.

Terror then reigned in Malaga, for the citizens understood that they could expect little mercy. Desperate, they sent a second deputation to Ferdinand's camp, through whom they suggested that the city should be surrendered to the conqueror with all its riches in exchange for the assurance that no harm should come to the citizens. Unless Ferdinand granted their request, they threatened, they would hang all the Christian slaves they possessed, and there were as many as six hundred of these in Malaga. They would also set fire to the town so that there would be no rich pickings for the invaders.

Ferdinand, however, was not inclined to bargain. If the Christian slaves were harmed, he replied, every inhabitant of Malaga would be put to the sword.

There remained nothing after that but for Ferdinand to force his way into the city. First he took the citadel, and above the city, for the first time for more than seven centuries floated the banner of Christian Spain.

The dead, who had been left to putrefy in the town, were then removed, the finest of the mosques was dedicated to Santa Maria de la Encarnacion, and Ferdinand with Isabella made their formal entry into the city.

Christian slaves were released from the dungeons, and when they came tottering forward to pay homage to the sovereigns Isabella wept and Ferdinand embraced them. The chains which bound them were removed, and a feast was ordered to be set before them. They were promised money and land.

Ferdinand then ordered the conquered commander, Hamet Zeli, to be brought to him. Before him stood the great chieftain, manacled and in chains, his head held high, his eyes flashing.

'You were foolish,' Ferdinand told him, 'to hold out against us. It would have gone easier for you and these people had you surrendered three months ago.' To which the brave Hamet Zeli cried out that his King had commanded him to defend Malaga, and if he had been supported he would have died before he surrendered.

Ferdinand shrugged him aside and declared he was ready to announce to the anxious people the punishment he had decided to inflict upon them. The entire population was to assemble in the great courtyard of the Alcazaba. There they were told their fate. All were condemned to slavery. One third was to go to Africa in exchange for Christian slaves held there. Of the remaining two thirds, half were the property of the state, which would use them as payment for the cost of the war; and the other half were to be given as presents to foreign friends, in Naples, Portugal and Rome.

The most fortunate were those who were sent to Rome – which seems ironical. Rome was the centre of the Catholic Faith, yet it is from Rome that we hear of leniency towards the Infidels. Innocent VIII put his slaves into the army and in a very short time, so we are told by the Curate of Los Palacios, made not only good soldiers, but good Christians of them. A comparison can be drawn between an *auto de fé* which took place in Rome under Alexander VI, and those hideous ceremonies which were becoming a commonplace in Spain. In July 1498 one hundred and eighty heretics (who had come from Spain after the great expulsion) were required to expiate their lapse into Judaism. Alexander watched the scene from St Peter's. The victims paraded in their *sanbenitos*, went through the formal ceremony of reconciliation to the Church, entered Santa Maria della Minerva, where they took off their *sanbenitos*, and afterwards went home to lead the lives of ordinary citizens, no further penance having been demanded of them.

This makes one pause to consider the difference in two men – Roderigo Borgia, Pope Alexander VI, and Torquemada. Alexander was a sensualist and a murderer, we know; he, with perhaps the exception of his son Cesare Borgia is the most notorious figure of his age; it has been said that he spent half his time performing his sacred duties as the Pope, and the other half with his mistresses in those orgies suited to his tastes. It is odd that he should have shown more kindness to the oppressed then did the saintly Torquemada. But it may have been because the worldly Alexander was a brilliant diplomatist, and Torquemada, for all his fervent devotion to Spain, a little foolish. When Torquemada banished the Jews from Spain, many of them found their way to Rome. They were the most fortunate section of the expelled community, for in Rome they were received with warmth. Alexander was clever enough to realize that they would help to enrich his domain.

The terrible fate of Malaga set panic raging throughout the Moorish Kingdom. A whole town condemned to slavery! This was how the Christians treated their prisoners. And Malaga was the port of Granada. How could the Moorish kingdom continue to exist without it?

The doom of the Mussulmans was close.

They knew it, and perhaps it helped to hasten their surrender.

But although Malaga was conquered in 1487 there was a great deal to do before the last battle was won. There followed the seige of Baza, which was ruled by El Zagal; and whilst this was in progress the Sultan of Egypt sent threatening messages to Ferdinand, warning him of Egypt's intervention if Christian persecution of the Moors did not cease. El Zagal was not so fortunate nearer home. Arms and men from Boabdil in Granada would have been more effective than threats from the Sultan of Egypt. But Boabdil was not a great fighter; he was a lover of peace and had already made certain terms with Ferdinand which aroused the wrath of his mother and many of the people, who declared he was a Christian in secret and that, for favours he had received from Ferdinand and Isabella, he was aiding their campaign against his own brethren.

Great hardship was suffered by Ferdinand's armies, and Isabella was constantly with the soldiers, caring for the sick, raising money to carry on the war, rousing the men to fresh enthusiasm, so that her presence in the camp was a necessity; and with her inspiration, Ferdinand's bravery, and the determination of both of them to succeed, they were, as they had said, one as important as the other.

Baza fell after a five months' siege, and the way lay open to Granada.

In 1490, the Infanta Isabella was married to Alonso, heir to the throne of Portugal, and the war against the Moors was suspended for a short while during which festivities took place. Isabella graced the fêtes and tourneys, and Ferdinand showed his dexterity with a lance; but Isabella mourned the loss of her daughter. She loved all her children dearly and, although she would not have dreamed of standing between them and the glory they could bring to their country, she suffered as a mother. But when the revelries were over, the sovereigns turned their attention to Granada; they sent for Boabdil, whose previous conduct had made him almost a vassal, to come to them and discuss terms.

Boabdil, however, showed unusual spirit. He had returned to Granada and was now among his people. He declared that he was not his own master and could not come when summoned by Ferdinand and Isabella.

Moreover the people of Granada now seemed to have taken heart. They had their backs to the wall and that knowledge seemed to infuse them with greater valour, greater determination to make the enemy pay for all he took.

There were skirmishes between the armies from which the Christians did not always emerge triumphant. Ferdinand marched against Granada then and, although he could not at that stage take the city he destroyed all the crops surrounding it; and it was during these operations that he bestowed knighthood on his little son, the Infante Juan, who was then twelve years old.

Granada itself was strongly defended. On the east was the defence of the Sierra Nevada; and where there were not natural barriers, the Moors had built great walls and fortifications to defend their capital city.

Ferdinand and Isabella were prepared for a prolonged resistance at the last stronghold, and they undertook the enormous task of building a town close to Granada in case they should be forced to stay in front of the city for some time. The armies had suffered hardship before Malaga and Baza; this should not be the case before Granada. It seems incredible nowadays to imagine the scene: soldiers turned into workmen, building busily in the midst of a war. The new town had two wide avenues made in the form of a cross; and when it was completed it was called Santa Fé on Isabella's request, although it had been suggested that the town should be named after her.

The sight of Santa Fé had a devastating effect on the morale of the Moors; they realized that the Christians had determined to blockade them out of existence.

Unfortunately for the Moors they had not a strong leader in Boabdil who, convinced that it would be impossible to hold out against the massing Christian armies, and no doubt eager to avoid for Granada the fate which had befallen Malaga, offered to negotiate for peace. This offer was accepted, although the people of Granada were unaware of it, as all communications between Boabdil and Ferdinand were conducted in secrecy. Meanwhile the people of Granada continued to prepare themselves for a long siege and were in high spirits, for they did not believe their friends in Africa would allow the last Moorish dominions to fall into the hands of the Christians; and daily they waited for the arrival of their allies.

Boabdil no doubt believed that by negotiation he could get the best for his people; and he was right in this, as was seen by the stubborn stand taken by the people of Malaga, the reward of which had been slavery. Boabdil asked that his people should be allowed to worship as they wished, and that their mosques in the city of Granada should be left to them; that , although they would be subjects of Isabella and Ferdinand, they should have their own *cadis* to administer laws which should be Moorish laws. They were not to be robbed of their property, but allowed to wear their traditional dress, use their own language and keep their customs. Boabdil would naturally be deposed, but he was to be given a small dominion in the Alpujarras which he would rule as a vassal of the Catholic Sovereigns.

When the citizens of Granada knew what Boabdil had arranged for them they rose against him, and such was his jeopardy that Ferdinand decided he would take immediate possession of the town and not wait until the date specified in the agreement.

The Spaniards were at this time mourning the death of Alonso of Portugal who had fallen from his horse; he was closely connected with the royal family since, a few months before, he had married the Infanta Isabella. But mourning was set aside and a glittering Spanish cavalcade accompanied Isabella and Ferdinand into Granada on the 2nd January, 1492.

This was the finest hour in Spanish history. It must have been a splendid and moving occasion when the Christian standard was placed on the towers of the Alhambra.

As for sad Boabdil, he made his way to the Alpujarras and from a rocky point – a spot which is still called The Last Sigh of the Moor – he looked back on Granada. It is said that he wept with great bitterness and that his mother, disgusted because he had bargained with the conquerors, made that often quoted remark: 'You do well to weep like a woman for what you could not defend like a man.'

One feels a little sorry for Boabdil who after all would have brought misery on his people had he fought bravely to retain what it was impossible to hold. He lived for a brief year in his poor little kingdom of the Alpujarras, and then, being unable to remain so near Granada and yet so far from it, he crossed the sea to Fez and very soon afterwards, helping an African kinsman in battle, he was killed. 'Wretched Boabdil!' it has been written of him. 'He lost his life in another's cause though he did not dare to die in his own.'

It was while they were in Granada that Ferdinand and Isabella signed the Edict which was to force to leave Spain all Jews who would not receive baptism.

For several years Torquemada had been urging the sovereigns to sign this Edict, but both Ferdinand and Isabella, deeply immersed in the war against the Moors, had hesitated. The Inquisition had disappointed them a little because of the amount of money it had produced. It was true that the confiscations brought in a great deal, but there were so many officers of the Inquisition, so many formalities, that a large proportion of the spoils was used up in the maintenance of the institution.

The Jews continued to grow richer, and it appeared that

most of the wealth of the kingdom was in their possession. They had an uncanny instinct for attracting wealth, and Isabella and Ferdinand were beginning to realize that to turn them out of the country could mean destroying that source of revenue which, in spite of centuries of persecution, seemed inexhaustible.

For this reason the sovereigns had so far refused to listen to the importuning of Torquemada and his adherents. But now they changed their minds. The La Guardia trial had sent a wave of hysteria through the country. Scandalous stories were circulated concerning the Jews: Their doctors carried poison under their fingernails, it was said, that they might kill the sick whom they were called to attend; the old story of the poisoned wells revived. Torquemada came to the Alhambra to see his sovereigns. The greatest event in Spanish history had recently taken place. The sovereigns had won the holy war, and as a result they had a chance of making all Spain Catholic. Yet they allowed these Jews to live in their midst.

Eloquent as ever, Torquemada raged against the Jews, nor did he spare his sovereigns. They must do their duty. They must expel the Jews.

As a result of his activities, the Edict was signed on the 31st March of the same year in which Granada had fallen.

The blow to the Jews, was, as can be imagined, catastrophic. They had suffered great cruelties for many years, but to be expelled from the only land which they could call home, to be forced to give up their property (for that was what it amounted to, as they, having to sell so quickly what they possessed, could be sure they would be paid very little for it; and in any case they were not allowed to take gold or silver out of the country) was the greatest misery, short of death, that could befall them.

Torquemada sent Dominicans into the *juderías*. He was very eager that it should be known that he did not wish so much to expel Jews as to convert them. If they were baptized they might stay in Spain. The dread Inquisition would naturally be a great shadow over their lives, for New Christians were constantly suspected of reverting to their old Faith; but at least they would not have to sell their house for an ass or their vineyards for a strip of cloth.

Against the Dominicans were the Rabbis, who urged their flock to remain true to the Law of Moses, reminding the people of how the children of Israel had been led from the land of Egypt. Thus appealed to, many decided to go rather than be forced to pretend to believe what was outside their belief.

But the Jews knew that Ferdinand needed money, and it occurred to them that, if they offered a large enough sum, they might ask in exchange for permission to stay in their homes.

So they sent a deputation to Ferdinand telling him that if the Edict could be destroyed the Jews would collect thirty thousand ducats and present them to Ferdinand as a donation towards the cost of the war.

When Ferdinand heard this his eyes glistened. Thirty thousand ducats was a sum not to be despised, and the wars had indeed been costly. Isabella was also attracted by the offer. She knew that the Jewish population was not only clever but hardworking, and she would be glad of an excuse to let them remain.

They were about to accept the offer when Torquemada, who had heard of the arrival of the deputation, burst in upon them.

He strode towards the King and Queen and with a dramatic gesture held up the crucifix which he always carried.

'Judas Iscariot sold his Master for thirty pieces of silver,' he cried. 'Your Highnesses are ready to sell Him anew for thirty thousand.' He threw the crucifix on the table and continued: 'Here He is. Take Him and barter Him. But do not think that I will have any share in such an odious transaction.'

Then he strode out of the room.

One might have thought that the two mighty sovereigns would have been angered by his insolence, but such was the power of Torquemada, such was his fire and eloquence, that both Ferdinand and Isabella thrust aside the tempting ducats.

The Edict should go forth.

The time for leaving arrived, and what a pitiful sight it must have been! Men, women and children – babies in arms among them – huddled together like a great army in retreat. Some had horses or asses on which to ride; but a great many must travel on foot.

Many of those who had shortly before called for riots against them were moved by pity at this terrible sight of so many homeless people, robbed of their possessions – for there was little they could take with them – wandering towards the coast, uncertain to what new land they would go.

It was however forbidden to help them. The Grand Inquisitor, Torquemada himself, had laid down a rule that any performing an act of neighbourliness towards these suffering people, would have committed an offence against the Church.

Some made their way to Portugal, for the King, John II, had, at a price, offered them a safe passage on their way to Africa. Some went to Italy, and those who arrived in Naples took the plague with them which decimated many of their numbers besides countless members of the existing population. Others landed in Genoa where they were not allowed to stay for, according to the law, no Jewish traveller must rest there for more than three days; but they were allowed to refit and replenish their ships, and when they went it was discovered that they had left the plague behind them.

Others found their way to Turkey and the Levant. Some went to France and a few to England.

Many found their way to Ercilla, a Christian Settlement in Africa, hoping to make their way to Fez; but desert tribes, hearing of their arrival and believing that Jews were always rich, came to meet them. Not content with robbing them, they violated the women and cut off the heads of any person who attempted to stop them. Some, believing that the travellers might have swallowed their valuables at the approach of danger, ripped up their bodies in the hope of finding them.

Those who were left struggled on without adequate clothing (for they had been robbed of all the good things they possessed), without food. They lived on the very small amount of grass which grew in the arid district; many died and the rest turned back to Ercilla, willing now to have the Christian Faith forced upon them for the sake of a little food.

There surely can be nothing more sad then to imagine these people who had bravely refused to swerve from their Faith and had undertaken the hazardous journey into the unknown. We are told that they waited at Cadiz and Santa Maria for the sea to divide for them as, so their scripture told them, it had divided for their ancestors.

The only fortunate Jews were those who went to Rome where, oddly enough that old sinner Roderigo Borgia Alexander VI (not out of his goodness of heart, but out of his wisdom), gave them a refuge.

So the Jews were expelled from Spain, and the Inquisition grew mightier yet. The fall of Granada was to bring in new victims. There would be those Moors who, as the Jews before them, would be forced to accept Christianity; and these *Moriscos* would very soon be found guilty of reverting to their traditional faith.

There were also the Protestants.

BIBLIOGRAPHY

Acton, John Emerich Edward Dalberg, First Baron Acton, D.C.L., LL.D., Edited with an introduction by John Neville Figgis, M.A., and Reginald Vere Laurence, M.A. *The History of Freedom* and *Other Essays*. (1907)

Aradi, Zsolt. *The Popes*. (1956)

Aubrey, William Hickman Smith. *The National and Domestic History of England*.

Bainton, Roland H. *The Reformation of the 16th Century*. (1953)

Bainton, Roland H. *The Travail of Religious Liberty*. (1953)

Baker, The Rev J., M.A. (Compiled and Translated by). *The History of the Inquisition as it subsists in the Kingdoms of Spain, Portugal, etc., and in both the Indies to this day*. (1734)

Berdyaev, Nicolas. With a Commentary and Notes by Alan A. Spears. Translated by Alan A. Spears and Victor B. Kanter. *Christianity and Anti-Semitism*. (1952)

Bertrand, Louis and Sir Charles Petrie, M.A., F.R.Hist.S. *The History of Spain*. (1934)

Bury, J. B. with an Epilogue by H. J. Blackham. *A History of Freedom of Thought*. (1952)

Butterfield, Herbert. *Christianity in European History*. (1951)

Cary-Elwes, Columbia, Monk of Ampleforth. With a preface by Professor Arnold Toynbee. *Law, Liberty and Love*. (1949)

Creighton, M., D.D. Oxon. and Cam. *Persecution and Tolerance*. (1895)

Dawson, Christopher. *Religion and the Rise of Western Culture*. (1950)

Deanesly, M., M.A. *A History of the Medieval Church, 590–1500*. (1925)

Gifford, William Alva. *The Story of the Faith*. (1946)

Gordon, Janet. *The Spanish Inquisition*. (1898)

Gowen, Herbert H., D.D., F.R.A.S. *A History of Religion*. (1934)

Guizot, M. Translated by Robert Black, M.A. *The History of France*. (1881)

Hope, Thomas. *Torquemada, Scourge of the Jews*. (1939)

Hume, Martin A. S. *Spain, Its Greatness and Decay (1479–1788) Cambridge Historical Series.* (1931)

Lea, Henry Charles, LL.D. *A History of the Inquisition of the Middle Ages.* 3 Volumes. (1887)

Lea, Henry Charles, LL.D. *A History of the Inquisition of Spain.* 4 Volumes. (1908)

Lea, Henry Charles, LL.D. *Chapters from the Religious History of Spain connected with the Inquisition.* (1890)

Lea, Henry Charles, LL.D. *Superstition and Force.* (1892)

Lea, Henry Charles, LL.D. *The Inquisition of the Spanish Dependencies.* (1908)

Limborch, Philip. *The History of the Inquisition.* (1816)

Marchant, John and others. *A Review of the Bloody Tribunal;* or the *Horrid Cruelties of the Inquisition as practised in Spain, Portugal, Italy and the East and West Indies.* (1770)

Maycock, A. L., M.A. With an Introduction by Father Ronald Knox. *The Inquisition from its Establishment to the Great Schism.* (1926)

McKinnon, James, Ph.D., D.D., D.Th., LL.D. *Calvin and the Reformation.* (1936)

McKnight, John P. *The Papacy.* (1953)

Mortimer, R. C., M.A., B.D. *The Elements of Moral Theology.* (1947)

Nickerson, Hoffman. With a Preface by Hilaire Belloc. *The Inquisition, A Political and Military Study of its Establishment.* (1923)

Poole, Reginald Lane. *Illustrations of the History of Medieval Thought and Learning.* (1880)

Prescott, William H. *History of the Reign of Ferdinand and Isabella the Catholic.* 2 Volumes.

Prescott, William H. *The History of the Reign of Philip the Second, King of Spain.* 3 Volumes (1873)

Robertson, John M. *A Short History of Freethought Ancient and Modern.* 2 Volumes. (1915)

Roth, Cecil. *The Spanish Inquisition.* (1937)

Rule, William Harris, D.D. *History of the Inquisition.* 2 Volumes. (1874)

Sabatini, Rafael. *Torquemada and the Spanish Inquisition.* (1928)

Shewring, Walter (Translated and Introduced by). *Rich and Poor in Christian Tradition.* Writings of many centuries. (1947)

Simon, Dr Paul. Translated from the German by Meyrick Booth, Ph.D. *The Human Element in the Church of Christ.* (1953)

Stephen, James Fitzjames, Q.C. *Liberty, Equality, Fraternity.* (1873)

Swain, John. *The Pleasures of the Torture Chamber.* (1931)

Turberville, A. S., M.C., M.A., B.Litt. *The Spanish Inquisition.* (1932)

Turberville, A. S., M.C., M.A., B.Litt. *Medieval Heresy and the Inquisition.* (1920)

Wiseman, F. J., M.A. *Roman Spain. An Introduction to the Roman Antiquities of Spain and Portugal.* (1956)

Essays by

Amado, Ramón Ruiz. *Isabella the Catholic.*

Amado, Ramón Ruiz. *Spain*

Bihl, Michael. *Elizabeth of Hungary called Saint Elizabeth.*

Blötzer, Joseph. *The Inquisition.*

Burton, Edwin. *Simon de Montfort.*

Callan, Charles J. *Rainerio Sacchoni.*

Kirsch, J. P. *Conrad of Marburg.*

O'Connor, John B. *Saint Dominic.*

O'Kane, Michael. *Raymond de Penaforte.*

Ott, Michael. *Innocent III.*

Ott, Michael. *Gregory IX.*

Ott, Michael. *Honorius III.*

Wilhelm, J. *Hus.*

All from *The Catholic Encyclopedia.* Edited by Charles G. Herbermann, Ph.D., LL.D.; Edward A. Pace, Ph.D., D.D.; Condé B. Pallen, Ph.D., LL.D.; Thomas J. Shahan, D.D.; John J. Wynne, S.J. Assisted by numerous collaborators. (1907)

INDEX

Ferdinand V (The Catholic), 9, 67, 88, 89, 91; Isabella promised to him, 97; birth, 100; appearance, 104, 106; marriage, 107, 108; wounded vanity, war of succession, 108; King of Aragon, 110, 111; controversy with Sixtus IV, 118; greed, 121–23; aids Inquisition, 125; protests from Sixtus, 133, 134; resents Papal interference with Inquisition, 139; war against Moors, 142, 147; understanding with Navarrese, 178; presides over Cortes at Taraçona, 181; appoints Inquisitors for Aragon, 182, 184, 185; condemns Malaga to slavery, 199; sends for Boabdil, 201; before Granada, 202; urged to expel Jews, 203; tempted by Jews, 205; resists temptation, 205

Flagellants, 41

Florinda, 77; raped by Roderic, 78

Flotte, Pierre, 45

Foix, Gaston de, marries Leonora, 100, 103

Foix, Gaston, de son of above, 103

Foulques, Bishop of Toulouse, gives aid to St Dominic, 32

Franciscans, 35, 51

Francis, St, founds Order, 28; character, 28; canonized, 35, 38, 120

Franco Brothers, 188, 189, 190

Franco, Ca, 188, 192; tortured and burned alive, 193, 194

Franco, Mosé, 187, 191

Franco, Yucé, 188; trial, 189; in prison, 190; confession, 191; tortured and burned alive, 193, 194

François I, of France, and the Vaudois, 53, 54, 55

Frederick II, of Sicily, 28; goes on Crusade, 34, 40

Garcia, Benito, brought before Villada, 187; in prison, 187, 190; executed, 191, 193

Gerard, Refugee from Germany, 62

Ghibellines, 56

Giron, Pedro, offered hand of Isabella, 97; mysterious death 98

Gnostics, 14, 17

Gondebaud, King of Burgundy, 72, 73, 74

Gregory VIII, Pope, 25

Gregory IX, Pope, 10; canonizes St Dominic, 29; election, 33; cleanses Rome, 35, 37, 41, 43

Gregory XI, Pope, election, 42

Gregory XII, Pope, determines to stop heresy, 58

Guelphs, 56

Guérin, 55

Gui, Bernard, 153

Guido, Cistercian Monk, 26

Guienne, Duke of, offers Isabella marriage, 99; suggested match with La Beltraneja, 107

Guzman, informs on New Christians, 121–22; 187

Guzman, Antonio de, 29, 30

Guzman, Felix de, 29

Guzman, Manes de, 29, 30

Hakam I, 84; burns Secunda and crucifies citizens, 86

Hamet Zeli, 197; in chains before Ferdinand, 198

Hannibal, 69

Hasdrubal (Son of Hamilcar), 69

Hasdrubal (Son-in-law of Hamilcar), 69

Hausrath, 39

Heisterbach, Caesarius, 39

Hélöise, Prioress of Argenteuil and Abbess of the Paraclete, friendship with Abélard, 15

Henke, 39

Henriquez, Frederick, Admiral of Castile, 105

Henriquez, Joanna (Mother of Ferdinand), birth of Ferdinand, 100; unpopularity, 102; fights for Ferdinand and death, 104

Henry II of England, conflict with Thomas a'Becket, 20

Henry III of England, 21; religious persecution, 62, 63, 64

Henry II of France, 55

Henry II of Leon and Castile, persecutes Jews, 113

Henry IV of Castile, conflict with John II, 92; character, 93; repudiates first wife and remarries, 94; summons Isabella and Alfonso to Court, 95, 96, 98; opposes Isabella's marriage with Ferdinand, 105, 107; reconciled with Isabella, dies, 107–8; 111, 136

Henry VI of Sicily, 28

Hermann I of Thuringia, 39

Hermengild, St, 75

Hisham, Caliph, 82

Hisham I, 84

Holinshead, 66

Honorius III, Pope, succeeds to Papacy, 24; death, 34, 35

Hus, Jan, translates works of Wyclif, 58; summoned to Council of Constance and burned alive, 60

Iberians, 67

Ibn, Habib, 82

Innocent III, Pope, heralds Inquisition, 10; elected, determines to stamp out heresy 17; rallies Catholic world against Albigenses, 19, 20, 21; death, 24; election, 25; ambitions, 28; character, 29; unimpressed by St Dominic, 31, 34, 35, 51

Innocent IV, Pope, 164

Innocent VII, Pope orders action against Hus, 58

Innocent VIII, Pope, delights in his children, 145; leniency, 199

Isabella I (The Catholic), 9, 89, 90, 91; birth, 92, 93; upbringing, 94–5; summoned to Court, 95; refuses suitors, 97; refuses crown, 99; speeds up plans for marriage, 105; marriage, 106; proclaimed Queen, 108; war of succession, 109; Castile and Aragon united, 110, 111; reluctant to establish Inquisition, 118; Conflict with Sixtus, 119, 120; determines to make country Catholic, 123–4; commands people to help Inquisitors, 125; appoints Torquemada Inquisitor-General, 134; impressed by Torquemada, 136; attitude to *conversos*, 139; war against Granada, 142, 147; ambitions, 178; conduct after Truxillo rising, 180, 185; before Malaga, 196–201; builds Santa Fé, 202; signs edict for expulsion of Jews, 203–4

Isabella, Infanta, married to Alonso of Portugal, 201; death of Alonso, 203

Isabella (Mother of Isabella the Catholic), 92

Isidore, Bishop of Seville, 76

Izan, Gumiel d', 29

Jaime, Infante, gives refuge to New Christian, 185; sentenced to penance, 185

James, St, 112

James I, of England, 158

Japhet (Son of Noah), 112

Jerome, of Prague, 58; burned at stake, 59

Jews, persecuted in England, 62–64; persecuted by Sisebut, 76–77; persecuted in Spain,

produces 'Instructions' 141–4; attitude to Clergy, 145, 146; hatred of Moors, 147; torture, 152, 153; *sanbenito*, 169, 170, 171; Inquisition in Castile, 180; Aragon, 181–6; seeks case against Jews, 188–94; plans expulsion of Jews, 195; compared with Alexander VI, 199; persuades Isabella and Ferdinand to eject Jews, 203–4; reproaches Isabella and Ferdinand, 183

Trajan, Marcus Ulpius, Emperor, declared Christians political danger, 12; gives succession to Nerva, 70

Trasimund, Count of Segni, 25

Tubal, 112

Urban III, Pope, 25

Urban V, Pope, despatches Dominicans to Germany, 41; death, 42

Val, Domingo de, victim of ritual murder, 113

Vaudois, massacre of, 53–4

Vaulx-Cernay, Pierre de, throws light on campaign against Albigenses, 23

Vaux, Pierre de (See Waldo, Peter)

Vergüenza, 154

Villada, Pedro de, treatment of Benito Garcia, 187, 188

Villena, Marquis of (Juan Pacheco), dominates Henry IV, 96; plans marriage between brother and Isabella, 96, 97; opposes Isabella's marriage with Ferdinand, 104, 105, 106; death, 108

Villena, Marquis of (son of above), supports La Beltraneja, 109

Vivero, John de, hospitality to Isabella, 106

Waldenses, 14, 15, 57

Waldo, Peter (Pierre de Vaux), theories, 15

Walid, Caliph, 80

Wenceslaus, 58

Wessel, Johann, 42

Wyclif, John attempts to reform Church, 58; Hus inspired by him, 59

Yahya ben Yahya, defies Hakam, 84; escape, 85

Yousouf, in conflict with Abd er Rhaman, 83

Zahara, favourite of Abd er Rhaman III, palace built for her, 86

Zoroaster, founds Parsee religion, 15

Zurita, Geronimo on Torquemada's possible Jewish blood, 138

GENERAL NON-FICTION

0352   Star

301392	Linda Blandford **OIL SHEIKHS**	95p
396121	Anthony Cave Brown **BODYGUARD OF LIES (Large Format)**	£1.95*
301368	John Dean **BLIND AMBITION**	£1.00*
300124	Dr. F. Dodson **HOW TO PARENT**	75p*·
301457	**THE FAMILY DICTIONARY OF SYMPTOMS**	95p*
398914	J. Paul Getty **HOW TO BE RICH**	60p*
397829	**HOW TO BE A SUCCESSFUL EXECUTIVE**	60p*
398566	Harry Lorayne & Jerry Lucas **THE MEMORY BOOK**	60p*
39692X	Henry Miller **THE WORLD OF SEX**	60p
395311	Neville Randall & Gary Keane **FOCUS ON FACT:** **THE WORLD OF INVENTION (illus)**	75p
39532X	**THE STORY OF SPORT (illus)**	75p
39529X	**THE PSYCHIC WORLD (illus)**	75p
395303	**THE STORY OF CHRISTMAS (illus)**	75p
395338	**UNSOLVED MYSTERIES (illus)**	75p
397640	David Reuben **HOW TO GET MORE OUT OF SEX**	85p*
398779	Fiona Richmond **FIONA**	50p
396040	Idries Shah **THE SUFIS (Large Format)**	£1.95
395478	Michael Smith **THE DUCHESS OF DUKE STREET ENTERTAINS**	£1.50 ◆

† For sale in Britain and Ireland only.
*Not for sale in Canada.
◆ Film & T.V. tie-ins.

0426 Universal/Tandem

	Thomas B. Costain **THE PAGEANT OF ENGLAND:**	
123190	1135-1216: THE CONQUERING FAMILY	£1.50
123271	1216-1272: THE MAGNIFICENT CENTURY	£1.50
123352	1272-1377: THE THREE EDWARDS	£1.50
123433	1377-1485: THE LAST PLANTAGENETS	£1.50
184033	Ben Davidson **THE OFFICIAL FONZIE SCRAPBOOK**	70p* ♦
08571X	Hyam Maccoby **REVOLUTION IN JUDAEA**	75p
168623	Xaviera Hollander **THE HAPPY HOOKER**	80p*
163443	LETTERS TO THE HAPPY HOOKER	80p*
168038	XAVIERA GOES WILD	80p*
166787	XAVIERA ON THE BEST PART OF A MAN	80p*
134265	XAVIERA!	80p*
17996X	Xaviera Hollander & Marilyn Chambers **XAVIERA MEETS MARILYN CHAMBERS**	80p*
124901	Fridtjof Nansen **FARTHEST NORTH**	£1.00
175158	Sakuzawa Nyoiti **MACROBIOTICS**	50p*
181638	Suze Randall **SUZE**	75p*
180755	Grant Tracy Saxon **THE HAPPY HUSTLER**	70p
134931	La Leche League **THE WOMANLY ART OF BREASTFEEDING**	60p
141970	Erna Wright **THE NEW CHILDBIRTH**	75p
067282	THE NEW CHILDHOOD	75p
054938	PERIODS WITHOUT PAIN	60p

0426 Hanau Distribution

087232	David Lewis **SEXPIONAGE**	70p
087151	THE SECRET LIFE OF ADOLPH HITLER	75p
086864	Linda Lovelace **INSIDE LINDA LOVELACE**	60p
086945	**THE INTIMATE DIARY OF LINDA LOVELACE**	60p
086007	Gerard I. Nierenberg & Henry H. Calero **HOW TO READ A PERSON LIKE A BOOK**	95p

† For sale in Britain and Ireland only.
*Not for sale in Canada.
♦ Film & T.V. tie-ins

BIOGRAPHY

0352	Star	
	General	(all are illustrated)

	Doris Day & A. E. Hotchner	
395680	**DORIS DAY, HER OWN STORY**	95p*
	The Duchess of Bedford	
398078	**NICOLE NOBODY**	75p
	Max Bygraves	
396091	**I WANNA TELL YOU A STORY**	70p
	Diana Dors	
301589	**FOR ADULTS ONLY**	95p
	Peter Douglas	
300833	**CLINT EASTWOOD: MOVIN' ON**	75p
	Eric & Ernie	
300000	**THE AUTOBIOGRAPHY OF MORECAMBE AND WISE**	60p
	Margot Fonteyn	
397071	**MARGOT FONTEYN**	75p
	J. Paul Getty	
395362	**AS I SEE IT**	95p
	Noele Gordon	
300299	**MY LIFE AT CROSSROADS**	50p
	W. A. Harbinson	
301171	**EVITA (Large Format)**	£1.95
	Elizabeth Harrison	
301120	**LOVE, HONOUR AND DISMAY**	85p
	Frankie Howerd	
39594X	**ON THE WAY I LOST IT**	85p
	David Pryce-Jones	
30149X	**UNITY MITFORD**	95p
	Rene Jordan	
396873	**STREISAND**	75p
	Hildegarde Knef	
39644X	**THE VERDICT**	95p
	Lord Longford	
301473	**KENNEDY**	95p
	Lilli Palmer	
396083	**CHANGE LOBSTERS AND DANCE**	95p
	Jean Plaidy	
395044	**MARY QUEEN OF SCOTS**	95p
	Barry Sheene	
301430	**THE STORY SO FAR . . .**	85p
	Tennessee Williams	
395583	**MEMOIRS**	85p

Wyndham Books are obtainable from many booksellers and newsagents. If you have any difficulty please send purchase price plus postage on the scale below to:

> Wyndham Cash Sales,
> PO Box 11,
> Falmouth,
> Cornwall.
>
> OR
>
> Star Book Service,
> G.P.O. Box 29,
> Douglas,
> Isle of Man,
> British Isles.

While every effort is made to keep prices low, it is sometimes necessary to increase prices at short notice. Wyndham Books reserve the right to show new retail prices on covers which may differ from those advertised in the text or elsewhere.

Postage and Packing Rate
U.K.
One book 22p plus 10p per copy for each additional book ordered to a maximum charge of 82p.

B.F.P.O. & Eire
One book 22p plus 10p per copy for the next 6 books, and thereafter 4p per book.

Overseas
One book 30p plus 10p per copy for each additional book.

These charges are subject to Post Office charge fluctuations